PERSUASION GAMES

PERSUASION GAMES

Will you persuade or be persuaded?

Learn the mind games of influence and
how to win them

GILAN GORK

Dedication

I dedicate this book to my parents, Avrille
and Monty, who have always been the most
incredible influences in my life.

———————————

Persuasion Games

Gilan Gork

Copyright © Gilan Gork 2015, Johannesburg, South Africa.

1st edition, 1st printing, 2015.

Published by Porcupine Press (in association with
Gork International).

ISBN 978-0-620-65861-4

Gilan Gork's website is: www.gilangork.com.

PORCUPINE PRESS

Contents

1: Let the Games Begin!

*"Tact is the art of making a point
without making an enemy"*

— Isaac Newton

A Fascinating Realm

Would you like to see something *amazing*?

Turn to the section of colour images on page 92 of this book. Look at the first photo, entitled 'Gilan Smile'.

Take a good look at the photo for about five seconds, and then come back here. It's okay, I'll wait for you.

* * *

Here's my question: what did you see in the photo? If you like, you can take another quick look before reading on.

You probably think you saw a photo of me holding a piece of paper on which I'd written the word 'NITE'. This is a perfectly good conclusion to come to. It's the conclusion *everyone* comes to. However, I can give you a solid, gold-plated guarantee that *you did not see what you think you saw*. Later on in this book, I'll explain what I mean. I think you'll find the truth rather amazing.

It's not just amazing — it has a lot to do with persuasion, which is the endlessly fascinating realm of this book.

Jobs, Dates and Teenagers

You are in the persuasion business whether you realise it or not. So am I, and so is everyone else. If this is not immediately obvious, let me mention a few examples of what I mean.

Have you ever tried to get someone to go out on a date with you, or to ask *you* out on a date ? Have you ever attended an interview to get a job, a better job or a raise? Have you ever haggled over the price of something or tried to get a better bargain? Have you ever tried to get your partner or a group of friends to see the movie *you* want to see or go to the restaurant you happen to prefer? Have you ever tried to get a teenager to tidy his or her room? (In my teenage years, my parents gave me a porcelain sign for my door: 'My room was clean yesterday. So sorry you missed it'.)

There's no getting around it: we are all persuading, and *being* persuaded, every day of our lives. Sometimes we're aware of it, sometimes not. Sometimes persuasion works very well, and on other occasions it fails miserably.

2

It's a fascinating subject, and one that has obvious links to countless different fields: from advertising to business negotiations, from the art of management to the even more delicate art of making sure that a first date isn't also a last one.

Fundamental Forces

Persuasion games have been my pursuit and my passion for a very long time. In my case, it's more than just a detached, academic interest. In my professional work, which I'll tell you about a little later, I *have* to be able to persuade people to do as I wish or else I don't eat — and I don't like to go hungry!

I'm intrigued by the persuasion techniques that work, why they work, and how to make them work better. I'm also interested in some of the techniques that *don't* work — and why people still believe in them.

In my opinion, it's fair to say that influence and persuasion are 'fundamental forces' of human society. To understand these forces is to understand a great deal about how people 'tick' and how we are all living our lives in a criss-crossing maze of persuasions and evasions all the time.

In this book, I'll be your personal tour guide through the fascinating realm of persuasion and influence, myth and reality. Among other things, I'll share some 'inside information' that will help *you* to be a more successful persuader. I'll also be talking about a very special group of people who could claim to be the unsung heroes of the persuasion business: professional psychics! More about them later.

And at some stage, I'll explain why you really, truly, honestly did *not* see what you thought you saw in that 'NITE' photo!

So, if you're ready... let the persuasion games begin!

Allow Me to Introduce Myself

My name is Gilan Gork. If you're from outside my native South Africa, that name probably looks a bit unusual. Even if you *are* from South Africa, it's *still* a little unusual! I've spent hours of my life pointing out that my name is not 'cork'. I sometimes think I could have saved a lot of time just by going with 'cork' and having done with it.

I do four things.

I entertain people by reading minds, shaping thoughts and predicting decisions. I don't know if that sounds like fun, but it is. As far as I'm concerned, the human mind is the most amazing thing in the world. We understand a lot about how it works, but there's still plenty of wonder and mystery to be found in the realm of the mind, which is what my shows are all about. By the way, if you want to know the secrets behind all my mind-reading demonstrations, they are all fully explained in the section starting on page 185.

My fascination with the art, science and mythology of persuasion led me to branch out into the world of corporate talks and training. These days, I spend a lot of my time teaching top business executives how to apply some of my skills to many typical business situations — in sales, management and leadership.

When I'm not entertaining people or coaching executives, I travel the world to meet other people who share my fascination with the workings of the mind, particularly in the areas of influence and persuasion. I am always learning, expanding my own knowledge and seeking out the best teachers on the planet to help me to refine my skills.

Finally, I do what I can to help people discover the power of their mind, and how to overcome problems like doubt, fear and uncertainty. I'm not a therapist, healer or guru, and I never try to be. Nonetheless, every once in a while I get the chance to show people they can find a way past their doubts and fears, and live life with a relaxed, happy and confident attitude. I might not do this every day or in every meeting, but when I do… it feels like a good thing to do.

So now you know me, and what I'm all about. Let's look at some of the terms I'll be using in this book.

Useful Clarifications

There are a few terms I ought to clarify before we go any further. This will avoid a lot of misunderstanding later on.

Influence

In this book, I use the word 'influence' to mean 'conveying a set of values by example'. You can influence someone without having any specific, direct interaction with them. Indeed, you can influence someone without even meeting them. For example, if you are a successful sportsman and you always make a point of competing honestly and fairly, and accepting defeat with good grace, you can influence a lot of youngsters who want to emulate your success and your professional conduct. Your values influence their values, and inspire them to follow your example.

Persuasion

I use the word 'persuasion' to mean 'the process of achieving aligned objectives'. If I want to sell a car, and you want to buy a car, I want to find a way to align our interests so that the transaction takes place and we both get what we want at the same time. Persuasion always involves some form of personal interaction, but this can take many forms — spoken words, written words, gestures, expressions, reasoned arguments, emotive appeals, subliminal cues, evocation of specific memories, use of colour and imagery... and so on. We will be looking at lots of different persuasion strategies later in this book.

Manipulation

I use the word 'manipulation' to mean 'the process of shaping human responses'. In normal usage, 'manipulation' sounds like a bad thing, doesn't it? We tend to think that if one person is manipulating another, that has to be wrong or at least questionable. However, 'manipulation' is actually a neutral term. Like the surgeon's knife, it can be used for good or bad, and it all comes down to the character, motives and intentions of the person involved. If a caring mother 'manipulates' her child to be aware of the dangers of crossing the street, and to always cross in a safe way, I doubt anyone would see anything wrong with that. I could give many other examples, but I'm sure you get my point.

Psychic

I use the word 'psychic' to mean 'someone who gives readings of any kind, about personality, destiny or fortune'. This term covers people who give tarot card readings, palm readings and other readings of that ilk. I am not going to get drawn into discussions about whether or not psychics are 'real'. Personally, I lean towards the prevailing *scientific* view, which is that there is, so far, no good reason to suppose that psychic powers are real.

However, this is not really a debate that greatly interests me, nor is it particularly relevant to this book. Perhaps the fairest and most even-handed summary is this: psychic powers are as real as you want them to be. For the purposes of this book, let's just leave it at that. Incidentally, most psychics are female, and so are most of their clients. For this reason, I will usually use the female pronoun for both.

Cold reading

I use this term to mean 'giving a reading (about personality, destiny or fortune) without any prior information about the person you are giving the reading to'. The alternative term is 'hot reading', which is where some prior knowledge or information is involved. I will not be referring to 'hot reading' anywhere in this book.

I will refer to the person who gives the reading as a psychic, a cold reader or a reader. These three labels are synonymous for the purpose of this book.

At the risk of labouring the point, whenever if I refer to 'cold reading' I am neither suggesting that the person giving the reading is a fake nor suggesting that she is not. I am simply asserting that she is giving the reading without any prior information about the client.

Mind / brain

If you have ever studied a bit of philosophy, you will know that it is possible to argue about the nature of the brain, the nature of the mind and the relationship between them for hours on end. For the purpose of this book, I'll use these terms as follows.

You have a mass of grey, squidgy stuff between your ears. This is your brain. The 'mind' is the label we give to the activity of the brain, insofar as we are aware of this activity or can comment on it. These definitions may not be sufficiently rigorous for the next international philosophy symposium, but they're good enough to see us through to the end of this book.

Now that we have clarified a few useful terms, we can take a look at our first group of persuasive strategies. By the way, I haven't forgotten about that 'NITE' photo you think you saw earlier. I promise we'll get back to it... all in good time!

2: The Persuasive World

*"We naturally awaken in others the same attitude
of mind that we hold toward them!"*

— Elbert Hubbard

First Steps

If you read minds for a living, like I do, one question is never far away. 'So, Gilan,' people say, 'how did you get into all this?'

So let's start at the beginning.

When I was nine years old I was on holiday with my family at a place called Shelley Beach on South Africa's south coast. One day it rained and rained, meaning I had to stay indoors and I was looking for something to do. My grandfather, Sam, pulled out a chessboard and started teaching me how to play. I wasn't all that keen, to be honest, but it was raining and I'd exhausted all my other options so I gave 'Gramps' my attention.

In our first game, Gramps did something that both annoyed me and intrigued me at the same time: he won the game with what's known as the four-move checkmate. This is exactly what the name suggests: a very sly way to win a game of chess in just four moves! We played a few more games, and I started to get a little better, but each time my Gramps somehow managed to win in just a few moves.

I learned two valuable lessons that day.

- You need to think more moves ahead than the other guy. If you can see what he's planning to do before he does it, you can block his plans.

- You can gain an advantage over your opponent by learning patterns of moves that he doesn't know about.

For me, that's where it all started. Since that rainy day, I've always felt there are parallels between games of chess and the persuasion games that we all play, all the time. If you learn the right moves and the right patterns, you can stay ahead of the other guy. Similarly, once you know the shortcuts in the human mind, persuasion becomes much easier — sometimes as easy as a four-move checkmate!

In this book, I can't teach you *everything* I know. It would take about twenty years and a lot of practice. But I can lead you on an interesting journey through some of the most important persuasive strategies that will help you in your personal, social and professional life.

Mind-reader for Hire

When I perform my mentalism shows, exploring the limits of what's possible with the human mind, I like to challenge myself. For example, I sometimes sit down before a show and make up a story about an imaginary journey, including details such as a particular city, a particular activity I might enjoy while I'm there, my room number and so on. I write this out and keep it handy for later reference.

In the course of my show, I get various people in the audience to mention things such as a city, an activity, a number and so on. They don't know it at the time, but I am secretly trying to make sure they name the same details as the ones in my story! For instance, if I have mentioned Athens in my story, I try to make sure that when I invite someone to just *think* of a holiday destination, they choose Athens.

There are various ways to do this. For example, the audience might not realise that during the early part of my show, I've been careful to mention several things typically associated with Greece and Greek culture. These subtle references, mentioned in passing, make it more likely that when I ask someone to think of a city, they will probably think of Athens. It can get even more subtle than that. My audience might think I said, 'Think of a city', but what I actually said — if you slowed it down — was, 'Think of ath ity'. I've already given them the 'Ath' part, without them even realising!

The Joy of Failing

I don't always succeed when I attempt these demonstrations. Most of the time, I manage to make people think what I want them to think and do what I want them to do. However, I do *occasionally* fail.

The curious thing about this is that my audiences often enjoy the show more when I fail than when I succeed! I could choose to feel a bit hurt by this — after all, it's like watching a tightrope-walker just in the hope that he might fall off! However, I can understand the sense of intrigue that people feel when I'm doing the things I do on stage. They are interested to see whether it's all sure-fire, and works every time, or whether I'm taking some real risks that may, or may not, pay off.

Let me set the record straight: I don't think anything I do is ever 'sure-fire'. The human mind is too complex, and people are ultimately too unpredictable, for me ever to take my results for granted. When I manage to get things to work on stage, I'm obviously pleased, since this is what I'm paid to be good at. But when things do occasionally go wrong, I console myself with the fact that I've chosen to work with the human mind, the most complex and wonderful thing in the known universe. This being so, the occasional misfire is both understandable and, I hope, forgivable. (If I wanted guaranteed results every time, I could just operate a cheese slicer all day.)

I find failure rather fascinating. It reminds me that persuasion is never a perfect science, where *this* strategy always produces *that* result. There is always the chance of something unexpected happening.

The truth is that persuasion is like many other subjects: the more you know, the more you realise how little you know. The more I learn about influence and persuasion, from countless different sources and teachers, the more I understand that I will never be able to persuade *all* the people, *all* the time, with a perfect record of success. I'm pleased about this. It means my chosen sphere of expertise never grows stale. There is always something else to learn, another twist to the tale.

Persuasion Everywhere

When I first developed my interest in influence and persuasion, my main aim was to share my passion and my interest with audiences who just wanted some entertainment. However, I soon realised that persuasion is *everywhere* — it permeates more or less every sphere of our lives: personal, social and professional. I soon took my interest far beyond the confines of the stage, and wanted to learn about persuasion in other spheres of life.

Eventually, I came to a realisation. Your effectiveness, in any area of your life, is directly proportional to your level of influence.

- Managers need to persuade their staff

- Salespeople need to persuade prospective customers

- Marketing experts need to persuade consumers

- Coaches need to persuade players

- Parents need to persuade children

The list is endless. I'm sure you can think of many examples of how influence and persuasion play a part in *your* life.

Charts and Hearts

To understand persuasion, we must first of all look at the difference between rational and emotional thinking.

We are all capable of rational, logical thought, although some are more capable than others. We all know that some people tend to have more 'logical' minds than others. Computer programmers, for example, *have* to think in very rigid, logical ways just to do their job. In everyday life, we apply a little logical thinking every time we want to make plans, solve a problem or figure something out. This is rational thinking; the kind of thinking that can be represented by arrows flowing logically around a chart.

Clearly, some things exist beyond the reach of mere logical thought — such as airlines and their business models. As someone who often travels internationally, I have come to the conclusion that every airline in the world takes some sort of secret oath to defy and despise logic, especially when it comes to their pricing structures. How can be cheaper to buy a return ticket and not use the second half than to just buy a one-way ticket?

Politics is another arena where, as far as I can tell, demonstrating any interest in logical analysis is regarded as a serious failing, like having poor personal hygiene. It leads to people being shunned and asked to leave the room so that the proper business of politics, such as name-calling and petty bickering, can proceed in the traditional lively and uninterrupted manner.

However, while most of us *can* manage a little logical thought when we have to, this is not our natural tendency. What we tend to do, unless forced to do otherwise, is think emotionally or, to put it more accurately, pursue the fulfilment of our perceived emotional needs.

That having been said, in the interest of accuracy let me add that cognitive illusions can arise that have nothing to do with your emotions. For example, suppose you see lots of references to the idea that the only man-made structure visible from space is the Great Wall of China. This isn't true, but if you hear it mentioned sufficiently often, and never hear a different view, you will come to think of it as true whether you want to or not. There may not be any emotion involved — you probably don't care either way about what is visible from space — but the illusion can take up residence within your mind all the same.

Predictably Irrational

Dan Ariely, in his excellent book *Predictably Irrational*, has this to say:

> *"My further observation is that we are not only irrational, but predictably irrational — that our irrationality happens the same way, again and again."*

This wonderful insight captures a very important aspect of persuasion. If a person *always* behaves irrationally, they are not susceptible to *any* form of persuasion. To try to persuade them in any particular direction would be like trying to predict a perfectly random number, which is impossible (this is what 'random' means).

However, if a person is *predictably* irrational, this changes everything! This predictability means we *can* persuade him — maybe not always with 100% success, but certainly more often than not. The predictability is the key.

To take a simple example, imagine someone in a store choosing which toothpaste to buy. He could base his choice on any number of sensible, rational considerations: how effective it is, whether his dentist recommends it, whether he's had good results with it before... and so on. However, suppose he chooses toothpaste based on entirely *irrational* factors, such as whether the package is blue or whether the brand name sounds similar to his dog's name. What's more, suppose he bases his choice on a *different* irrational factor every time.

In this situation, and assuming I don't know anything about this strange man and his bizarre selection criteria, I lack any way to persuade him to buy my particular brand of toothpaste. If I tried, I would be likely to base my persuasive efforts on one or more of the *rational* factors listed above, such as handing out promotional leaflet saying my particular brand comes very highly recommended by the dental profession. This attempt would fail.

Even if I realised he always bases his choice on *irrational* factors, I still can't win because he uses different selection criteria every time.

Ah... but now consider the situation where I know he *always* bases his choices on the packaging, and his favourite colour is blue. It's still irrational, in the sense that the packaging has nothing to do with the merits of the toothpaste. However, it is *predictably* irrational. All I have to do to win the persuasion game is make sure the packaging is predominantly blue.

You might think this is just a silly hypothetical example, and in one sense it is. But imagine that instead of analysing how one (rather strange) man chooses toothpaste, we study the choices made by millions of people. We may well find that a high percentage make *predictably irrational* choices.

Minty Fresh?

This is the kind of thing that marketing experts study all day, and it explains why many brands of toothpaste have a minty flavour. The mint flavour tells you nothing about the merits of the toothpaste and whether it's doing your teeth any good. It's quite possible for a substance to taste 'minty fresh' and be about as good for your teeth as a chewing on pebbles. But consumers tend to like that minty taste, so the manufacturers put it in.

It's also why most shampoo products contain agents that produce plenty of lather and foam. The lather makes no difference to how well the product cleans your hair, and it's possible to create an excellent shampoo that hardly produces any lather at all. However, most consumers tend to associate lots of rich, foamy lather with powerful cleansing, and the shampoos that have this property sell better than the ones that don't.

This naturally leads to two interesting questions.

- How can you use this sort of knowledge to be influential and persuasive?

- How can you use it to prevent others from influencing and persuading you?

We will return to both of these questions many times in the course of this book.

A Million Messages

It is clearly the case that lots of people *want* to influence and persuade you every day. When you consider all the messages you deal with from TV, radio, websites, billboards, email, texts, telemarketers, customers, colleagues, your boss, charity appeals and so on, it's amazing that you make it through the day without screaming for it all to stop.

A given percentage of all these messages are from people and organisations that want to persuade you or manipulate you to suit their own ends. Sometimes they have good intentions, sometimes not; sometimes their persuasive techniques are rather open, sometimes rather subtle and sneaky. Nobody likes to think of themselves as a puppet, pulled by the strings of a clever advertising campaign or a calculated political appeal to your feelings. However, defending yourself from all of these many and various forms of persuasion is not easy. The advice I tend to give is always the same. In many sports, people say the best defence is a good offence. Similarly, if you don't want to be persuaded, *become a good persuader.*

In this book, I'll help you to become a good persuader. One of the reasons I can do this is that I've taken the time to learn from the best. Among other experts, I've tried to learn from the people I regard as the 'superheroes' of persuasion games. Let me tell you about them.

Masters of Persuasion

My desire to learn from various persuasion experts has taken me to some wonderful places and led to fascinating encounters with a wide range of people — some of whom I'm not *officially* allowed to mention.

My research eventually led me to a group of people who can legitimately claim to be some of the world's leading experts in persuasion, even though they are seldom given any credit for this.

I'm referring to psychics. More specifically, I mean people who can sit down with a client — a complete stranger they have never met before — and give her a twenty-minute reading that seems to be a reasonably accurate summary of that person's life, career, hopes, dreams, problems and relationships, all topped off with predictions about the future which later come true!

It doesn't really matter whether you believe in this sort of thing or not. Even if you take the view that psychic readings are hogwash, there's still plenty to admire about this process. Consider the challenge of meeting someone *you have never met before in your life,* and trying to talk to her for twenty minutes so she goes away believing you know more about her life than she does herself! Even if you view psychics in the most cynical way possible, this is still an intriguing phenomenon and one that I have studied for years.

An Old Debate

Before exploring this area any further, I'll just repeat a point I made in the earlier section called 'Useful Clarifications'.

This book is not about whether psychics are 'real' or not. This is a very old debate, and it's not one that has much bearing on our journey together to explore the world of persuasion. There *may* be some genuine psychics somewhere. That's a matter of conjecture. However, it is a matter of *fact* that some people do their 'psychic' thing via other means, relying on smart psychological techniques to deliver what seem to be impressively accurate psychic readings. In this book, I am exclusively concerned with the latter group.

It is not my purpose to 'debunk' these people or to dismiss them as charlatans. I'll let others take up that kind of battle cry. I know that really good psychic readers can convince just about anyone that they know everything about them. This is a skill I greatly admire. I try to learn all I can about how it's done and what lessons these people can teach the rest of us about persuasion and persuasive illusions.

Hot and Not

Within the psychic industry, there are two main schools. The first are the so-called 'hot readers', which means they secretly obtain information about their clients before they start giving the reading. There are countless ways to do this, and as a professional mentalist it's part of my job description to know how to get information by stealth. However, these methods must remain in the shadows for now.

The second group are known as 'cold readers', meaning that they give their readings *without any advance knowledge or information whatsoever*. They are, so to speak, going in 'completely cold'. It was this second group that fascinated me the most.

You might suspect that the people who are really good at this sort of thing don't tend to talk about their methods very much, and you would be right. However, I went to see some people, made some connections and eventually found my way to the leading expert in this field: Ian Rowland, who is based near London, England. Ian wrote the definitive book on cold reading and is also the only man in the world who has proved for the media, under *test conditions*, that cold reading really works. Luckily for me, he's also perfectly open about the subject and even allows people to study with him (which I did).

Ian doesn't earn a living posing as a psychic (although I'm sure he could if he wanted to). He's a writer and trainer, and among other things he teaches Applied Cold Reading, or ACR for short. This is about taking some principles of cold reading and applying them to fields outside the psychic industry, such as management, sales, teaching and therapy.

I was initially rather sceptical about ACR, since I couldn't fathom how someone seeing tall, dark strangers in a crystal ball had much in common with boardroom executives negotiating a new software contract. As it turned out, I was pleasantly surprised to discover just how many parallels there are, and how many of the psychic's psychological and verbal techniques can help anyone in the persuasion business. I got to know Ian quite well, and I enjoyed his many demonstrations of how cold reading works either within the psychic industry or outside it. His ability to make seemingly accurate statements about things he knows nothing about is beguilingly impressive, not to mention entertaining and, at times, very funny. (In the interests of full disclosure, I ought to add that I also asked Ian to give me a hand putting this book together, in his capacity as a professional writer and consultant.)

My interest in cold reading fuelled my interest in persuasion games of all kinds. I started noticing parallels between the persuasive techniques used in the psychic world and those found in advertising, marketing and other spheres. I will return to this theme throughout this book.

Gilan's Persuasion Tips

Here are three simple tips for you based on this chapter.

- Be aware that you are playing persuasion games all the time, and you can choose to either be persuader or persuaded.

- Remember the chess story, and look for the patterns that give you the persuasive advantage.

- Recognise the difference between wholly irrational behaviour (no persuasion possible) and *predictably* irrational behaviour (some persuasion possible).

Summary

In this chapter, I've shared a little about how I started my journey into the fascinating realm of persuasion, and how my interest in one persuasive arena (reading minds on stage) led to my interest in many other areas. We've touched on one crucial aspect of persuasion, which is the difference between rational, irrational and emotional thinking. We have also briefly met a rather secretive group of persuasion experts: cold readers, and their 'almost psychic' talents! We will be seeing a lot more of them later on.

What we have *not* done in this chapter is make any reference to the 'NITE' photo that I invited you to look at right at the very start of this book. I stand by what I wrote earlier: you did *not* see what you *think* you saw. I will explain everything a little later on.

In the next chapter, we'll take a look at one of the most important persuasive techniques in the world. It all starts with a lesson from a herring gull…

3: Fixed Response Patterns

"Character may almost be called the most effective means of persuasion."

— *Aristotle*

Chicks and Clicks

A herring gull chick demonstrates a remarkable pattern of behaviour. Whenever it sees the red dot on its mother's beak, it opens its own beak as wide as possible and clamours to be fed. This seems to be an entirely automatic response. If you show the chick something that is very similar to the red dot on its mother's beak, even just a dot painted on a stick, it will respond the same way every time.

Here's another example of the same amazing phenomenon. A female turkey will take anything under her wing that emits the characteristic chirping sound made by baby turkeys. Even if you wire a small transmitter inside something that bears no relationship to a turkey whatsoever, and play the recorded 'cheep cheep' sound of a turkey chick, the mother will treat the object like one of her young. This even works with a stuffed toy of one of the turkey's natural predators!

These are just two examples of the way animals have evolved to respond in a fixed, automatic way to specific stimuli, and there are many others.

This fixed response to a stimulus is called an FRP, or fixed response pattern. It doesn't involve any logic or conscious thought process as such: the stimulus triggers the same response every time, and it seems to be something the animals cannot control or override. Without straying too far into anthropomorphic thinking, it seems fair to say the animals are not even *aware*, in any meaningful sense, of the FRPs. From our point of view, it's as if the response is 'hard-wired' into the animal: you present the stimulus, you get the response.

People Patterns

Knowing that some animals exhibit a fixed response pattern (FRP) gives rise to an obvious question: does the same apply to people?

The answer is… yes and no. I am not aware of any human FRPs that are quite as simple and direct as, say, the herring gull example. And it's certainly the case that people don't *want* to be thought of as simply responding automatically to stimuli — people like to think they are thoughtful decision-makers, not puppets of their own built-in drives.

Nonetheless, it is possible to influence and modify human behaviour so that you can achieve what is, *in effect*, a fixed response pattern.

This should come as no surprise, since you are surrounded by examples every day. You know that if people feel passionately loyal to a given sports team, then the promoters only have to announce that tickets are on sale for the next big fixture and the fans will flock to buy those tickets as rapidly as possible — ignoring the distinct possibility that the game might turn out to be rather dull.

The same goes for fans of those singers and musicians who reach the very top of the show business ladder — as soon as the star's new tour is advertised, the fans go crazy to obtain tickets even though *at the time* they have absolutely no way of knowing whether the show they get to see will be any good. It's true that the star's track record, previous tours and cascade of hits suggest the show is *likely* to be good, but it's still not a given. (Tales of disappointment and regret are not uncommon, and often feature in the comments section of online reviews.)

Let's take a closer look at the fixed response patterns of everyday life.

Pick a Picture

If you turn to the section of colour images on page 92 of this book, you'll see a graphic entitled 'Choose 1 from 5'. Take a look at the row of five pictures and just choose one. There's no right or wrong answer, and you can choose whichever image you want.

When you have chosen one of the five pictures, you can continue reading this chapter.

I will assume that you have had a look at the 'Choose 1 From 5' graphic, and have chosen one of the five pictures.

Amazingly, I know *for sure* that you selected the picture of the tree! Isn't that amazing?

Actually, no, that's not true. I just wrote that to momentarily surprise and impress those of you that *did* choose the tree. If you were one of them, I hope you enjoyed that intriguing moment.

The fact is, I can't tell you which of the five images you selected. What I *can* tell you is that a very high percentage of you will have chosen either number 2 (teddy bear) or number 4 (puppy). Don't worry if this didn't work for you — it doesn't work for everyone, all the time.

Why does it work for most people, most of the time? The images at the extreme ends of the line, in other words 1 and 5, are perceived as being too extreme and a bit obvious, and to a lesser extent the same is true of the image that is precisely in the middle. Options 2 and 4 feel more like a free, independent choice that nobody could predict!

Just by way of a side note, whenever I try this demonstration in my live lectures, those who did *not* choose the second or fourth image tend to have a certain 'smug' look about them, as if they are proud to have demonstrated that they are not so easily led or manipulated. I usually get a laugh by pointing out that, in purely *statistical* terms, all they have done is demonstrate that they are 'not normal'!

People Reading

In my stage shows, I often have to size people up quickly and assess whether they are likely to do things the conventional way (like choosing image 2 or 4) or be a little more challenging and independent (like choosing one of the others). There are several subtle ways that I can go about this.

For example, when I welcome someone to the stage, I may hand them a simple prop such as a book. If the spectator automatically takes the book and holds it the correct way to open it and read it, even though I haven't asked him to, I know he tends to think along conventional lines. On the other hand, if he holds the book the 'wrong' way up or in an unconventional way, then it's safe to say he is less governed by conventional patterns of thought, expression and behaviour.

It's possible to use some of the same strategies in the world of business. For example, when you first meet someone, you can do something as innocent as asking them to pass you a pen. There is a conventional way to hold a pen, as you would if you were going to write with it, and plenty of other, unconventional ways that make no reference at all to the pen's actual function. If someone instinctively turns the pen around and holds it as he would for writing, then he is a 'conventional' thinker who probably thinks along preset lines. If not, then the opposite is probably true — he is an independent thinker who either isn't aware of the conventional way of doing something, or *is* aware and enjoys going against the grain and rejecting the metaphorical shackles of whatever is deemed to be the 'conventional' approach.

Accessing Agreement

FRPs can be very useful when you want someone to agree or co-operate with you. If you ask someone to do something, and offer a slight but modestly pleasant smile and nod, they feel inclined to do the same. This elicits a mood of agreement and co-operation.

You can try this out for yourself. Suppose that you need to ask someone to perform a relatively menial task. If you just say, 'Please take some spare notepads to the meeting room', they may comply or they may object and say why it's not their job or that they have better things to do. If you make the same request but add the friendly smile and the nod, you are far more likely to get a co-operative response.

Copycats

Harvard psychologist Ellen Langer once devised a simple experiment to do with a queue of people waiting to use a photocopier. She got students to see what happened if they asked to 'jump the queue' so they could do their copying before everyone else.

She found that if the student simply asked to go first, other people waiting in line would often refuse and insist on everyone taking their turn. However, if they asked to go first and *gave a reason*, they were almost always allowed to go to the front of the line. Here's the crucial part: the reason didn't have to be a good reason, or even to make sense. The student could say, 'Can I go ahead of you please, because I want to use the copier', and nine times out of ten they were allowed to do so. Just hearing the word 'because' led most people to think there was a good reason to give way.

If the other people in the queue had thought for a moment, and actually focused on what was being said, they would have noticed that 'because I want to use the copier' isn't actually any sort of reason or explanation at all why one person should take priority — *everyone* is there to use the copier! But they didn't. They had something close to an FRP that said, 'because = good reason/justification'.

Cold Patterns

My favourite persuasion experts, the cold readers, use FRPs a lot in their work. Let's look at this in some detail.

The human mind strives to find patterns in experience. This is a fundamental aspect of intelligence, and vital to the survival of each individual, tribe or society. Only by spotting patterns can you learn to communicate, walk, eat, move towards good things that are useful or pleasurable and away from harm or danger. British hypnotist and therapist James Tripp sometimes refers to people as 'meaning makers', which is a phrase I like.

Some writers in this area say it's as if the brain is 'preprogrammed' or 'hard-wired' to seek patterns in data and experience. This kind of terminology is misleading and can do more harm than good — the brain is not really like a computer, and to suggest that it is can lead to significant misunderstandings. However, without getting hung up on the particular terms or metaphors we use, it's clear that the human mind constantly seeks to identify and remember patterns in data.

The Triggered Response

Good cold readers take advantage of this by doing something that is quite simple yet remarkably effective: they explicitly trigger the mind's pattern-recognition ability. For example, consider a fairly standard situation in which a psychic is looking at a spread of tarot cards and giving her client a reading. She might offer a statement such as, 'There are indications here of a conflict or disagreement, involving your career but also a family member, and I think this situation could have been developing for some time. What is this in relation to?'

In the context of a psychic reading, this *sounds* as if the psychic is giving some factual information and then asking the client to verify how this relates to his or her life. In point of fact, the psychic is offering some vague, generalised phrases that could mean a thousand different things, and inviting the client to try to find a pattern — i.e. a way to relate any part of the statement to any part of her life. Note that the connection does not have to be perfect, or comprehensive — a partial match, or even a very slight one, will do perfectly well!

Some extra subtleties that can disguise this process even further. For example, if the psychic says, 'Can you relate to this?', the client might notice that she is being asked to find a link, *any* link, between what the psychic just said and her own life. However, the psychic can make this a little less obvious. After her two or three phrases about conflict, career and family, she can say, 'Now, does this apply specifically to you or to someone else that you've been thinking of lately?'

As soon as the client starts to evaluate this question and form an answer, she has *tacitly accepted* the task of finding a connection between what the psychic said and her own life, even though *she hasn't directly been asked to do so*. The invitation (please try to find a connection) and the acceptance (yes, okay, I will) are both unspoken and implied, rather than stated outright. This helps to make the technique less conspicuous.

Unspoken Truth

Given that fixed response patterns are very much in evidence in many aspects of human life, it is perhaps rather surprising that more people aren't aware of this, or not prepared to acknowledge it. The reason is fairly obvious: people cling to the notion that they are thoughtful, purposeful individuals who make their own choices, and do so in a way that seems reasonable. The idea that they may be governed by an FRP is uncomfortable for most people. It goes against their sense of identity and individuality.

Persuaders can exploit this reluctance to admit that our choices are not always as free from outside influence as we like to think. It creates the opportunity for some subtle flattery.

Consider the example of a car salesman aiming to sell a car to a customer. Let's suppose for a moment that the car really isn't all that great, but it is superficially attractive and attention-getting: a nice design, a bright red colour, some gleaming chrome components and an impressive top speed. Let's say the salesman is aware that the customer is probably easily impressed by all these superficial features. The salesman can say to the prospective buyer, 'I can see you're not the sort of man who's going to be easily impressed by superficial things like the colour, the top speed and so on...'

In saying this, the salesman is achieving several things. First of all, it gives him a chance to recite the list of superficial features that he is secretly aware the customer finds appealing. Secondly, he is giving the customer a little ego stroke, and appealing to his idealised sense of himself as someone who makes thoughtful, objective decisions unaffected by superficial traits. Thirdly, he gives the customer permission (mentally) to notice all of these superficial features again — because he can now do so without any sense of guilt that he finds such features appealing. He has been 'absolved' of the crime of being easily lured by trivial details, and reassured that he's not that sort of person (even though in fact he is, and the salesman is delighted that he is).

Miracles of Mind

I sometimes use a similar ploy in my stage work. I can't give away *all* my secrets in this book, but I don't mind giving you a brief glimpse into how I perform my 'miracles of mind'. (Just promise me that you'll keep the information to yourself and not tell anyone else.)

From time to time in my shows I may invite someone in the audience to choose a number between 1 and 20. If I just say, 'Please choose a number between 1 and 20', I am exerting very little influence over which number he will choose. Of course, I might still be able to *guess* which one he will choose. Being good at guessing is one of my essential professional skills.

However, consider this slightly different wording: 'Please choose a number between 1 and 20. I sometimes get people I can persuade to think of an extremely low or high number, like 2 or 19, but I can tell you're a bit more thoughtful than that.'

By saying this, I can be pretty confident the spectator will give me a number somewhere near the middle of the range I indicated, such as 9 or 11. By flattering him, and saying he's *not* the sort of person who could be easily manipulated, I am, in fact, manipulating his responses.

Free Will?

All the aspects of FRPs that we have looked at so far lead to an interesting point. In philosophical circles it is known as the debate between free will and determinism.

The 'free will' faction maintain that there *is* such a thing as free will, that a person can make his or her own choices and do so in a manner that is intrinsically unpredictable and non-deterministic. External factors may *influence* a decision, but the individual can always override them if he wishes to do so.

The 'determinist' faction claim the opposite: every decision a person makes is wholly determined by the preceding set of stimuli and events, just as the moon causes the tides. They say that 'free will' is just wishful thinking, a desire for there to be a 'ghost in the machine', to borrow Arthur Koestler's famous phrase.

The determinist says that if we were able to track every single relevant factor leading up to someone making a decision, we would, in theory, be able to predict which decision he or she will make. In practice, we seldom have access to all the relevant data or the ability (with current technology) to do the necessary calculations. Determinists say this is just a technical limitation, but their theoretical argument still stands.

This is a theme I love to play with in my shows. Sometimes, I ask a member of the audience to think of a movie star — any movie star at all, past or present. Let's say she says Marlon Brando. I ask her whether this was a free choice, or whether it was determined by external influences? She says it was a perfectly free choice. I then show everyone a brief video clip of the waiting area outside the theatre, where this particular spectator was waiting for two or three minutes along with everyone else. I show that:

- I planted several inconspicuous pictures of Marlon Brando all around this area.

- The music playing very quietly in the background was 'The Theme from the Godfather'.

- There was a fake advertising poster featuring a model who bears a resemblance to the late, great Mr Brando.

Just for an added twist, I point out that the letters 'MB' are printed, in very faint grey text, on the tickets to the show, and that some very small text says the show is produced by Odnarb Productions (try reading it backwards).

I'm not a philosopher and I don't know if we all have free will or not in any ultimate sense. What I *do* know, with certainty, is that we are all affected by external factors and influences *some* of the time, and often without being aware of it. I am very pleased that this is the case, or else I'd be out of work.

Gilan's Persuasion Tips

Here are three simple tips for you based on this chapter.

- Be on the lookout for fixed response patterns — the ones that may affect you, and the ones that might affect the people you want to persuade.

- To be persuasive, learn from the cold readers: see if you can trigger the other person's innate 'pattern recognition' faculties, and do so without making this explicit.

- Remember the car salesman example: If you want to exploit an FRP, mention it and tell the other person that you know they would never be affected by it.

Summary

In this chapter, we've looked at many different aspects of fixed response patterns, or FRPs. We've seen how most of us either aren't aware of our own FRPs or prefer not to acknowledge the role they might play in our choices and decisions. We also saw how this relates to a technique used by psychics: deliberately triggering the mind's pattern-recognition ability so that could-mean-anything statements actually sound meaningful.

I think it's a good idea to at least *try* to be aware of whatever FRPs play a role in your life, and recognise those times when you might behave in a rather predictable, preconditioned way rather than thinking things through properly. This is a very good defence against your FRPs being used against you. I'm sure you would rather be a thoughtful individual than the equivalent of a herring gull chick responding to a red dot.

However, even if you manage not to be affected by fixed response patterns, you will be fooled, misled and betrayed by another aspect of your mind, and this is what we'll look at in the next chapter. Have you ever planned a journey and then spotted a convenient shortcut? Well, your mind is doing this *all the time*. But shortcuts, as we will see, are sometimes a very bad idea.

4: Heuristics

"Not brute force but only persuasion and faith
are the kings of this world."

— *Thomas Carlyle*

Sex, Shoes and Cues

When you want to get somewhere quickly, it helps if you know a little shortcut. The same is true when it comes to thinking. There are such things as mental shortcuts, and they have two fascinating properties:

- you couldn't survive without them; and

- they can be *seriously* misleading.

These mental shortcuts are known as 'heuristics' (a word that comes from the same root as 'eureka'). For our purpose, we can define heuristics as 'a strategic approach that sacrifices accuracy for speed'.

You use heuristics all the time, and here's the proof. What do you think you are looking at here?

You probably think you are looking at a smiling face that just happens to be upside down. However, if you turn this book around for a moment, you'll soon see that this is most certainly *not* the case! The face is actually rather grotesque. Nonetheless, as soon as you turn the page the right way round again… your brain will still tell you that you're looking at a 'normal' face, just upside down.

This illusion was devised by British psychologist Peter Thompson. He called it 'The Thatcher Illusion', because the first version he prepared featured a photo of the late British Prime Minister Margaret Thatcher. However, the illusion works with any face, famous or not.

What's going on here? When you look at this picture you could, if you really needed to, study it closely enough to see that it's not quite what it appears to be, and that the eyes and mouth have been digitally altered. However, this would take up great deal of your brain's processing power. Your brain tries to conserve its processing power as far as it can, because this is a good survival strategy: it's good to keep some brain power in reserve in case a threat suddenly turns up out of nowhere.

For this reason, if you feel you can fairly safely solve a problem *without* using up a vast amount of brain power, you do. In this case, since you have been recognising human faces literally since the day you were born, you feel pretty confident about when you're looking at a face as opposed to looking at something else. When you looked at the picture, your brain noticed a few details associated with human faces — roughly oval shape, hair, two eyes, nose, mouth, jawline — and concluded it was a smiling face. It took a shortcut that would, under normal circumstances, work perfectly well.

However, on this particular occasion, I exploited the heuristic by presenting just enough clues to mislead it. For this reason, you came to a slightly erroneous conclusion (smiling face) instead of the correct one (grotesque image of an unreal, distorted face).

Heuristic Hazards

The 'distorted face' picture shows us that heuristics can lead to false conclusions, especially when they are deliberately derailed by misleading cues. However, they can lead to misleading conclusions even in the absence of any intentional deception.

Some people are very good at estimating things such as distance, size or how long it will take to complete a particular errand. Other people are hopeless at such estimates. Why? Because they happen to be employing heuristics that aren't very refined or sophisticated.

Plainly, familiarity and practice affect the dependability of any particular heuristic. A carpenter who works with wood every day of his life can probably tell you how long a plank is, very precisely, just by looking. His heuristic for 'estimate the length of a piece of wood' has had plenty of opportunity to evolve and improve. Give the same problem to someone who has never had to do this in his life before, and he'll probably give a hopelessly inaccurate answer.

You are using heuristics all the time — good ones honed by experience, and bad ones that can lead you astray and cause problems (such as arriving late for an important meeting because your 'estimate' of how long it would take you to get there was hopelessly inaccurate). In fact, you have no choice. Your brain is bombarded by stimuli all the time, and commercialism only exacerbates the problem. You see hundreds or even thousands of adverts and promotional messages every day.

If you had to stop and think about every single message, every little piece of data, then your brain — wonderful as it is — would simply be unable to cope. You *have* to apply heuristics, and accept the inevitable trade-off: faster processing speed and the ability to handle all the incoming data, at the expense of errors and reduced reliability.

Baiter and Baited

Heuristics are very important when it comes to persuasion games. At the risk of repeating myself, remember that heuristics have this intriguing dual nature:

- you couldn't survive without them; and

- they can be *seriously* misleading.

This means that the artful persuader, wishing to exploit heuristics, has to try to do two things at once:

- exploit the flaws of the not-very-good heuristics; and

- not get caught by the heuristics that work very well.

The Baiting of Clicks

To show you what I mean, let's look at a phenomenon instantly familiar to anyone who has spent so much as ten minutes on the Internet: clickbaiting. You can't spend much time browsing the Web without seeing dozens of short, punchy headlines intended to be so compelling or intriguing that you feel you *have* to click on them and see the full story. This is an advertising strategy, pure and simple. Many commercial websites rely on clickbait to attract traffic and thereby increase their chances of selling either their own products or those of the companies who pay to place ads on their site.

Clickbait headlines work by placing simple, clear and (apparently) interesting ideas in front of you. In effect, they are saying, 'There is a lot of clutter all over the Internet, but here's something fun and interesting that's easy to understand.' They appeal to your heuristic that says, 'Try to filter out the clutter and just find something worth reading.'

This is where it gets interesting. You *also* have a heuristic that says, 'Avoid things that are just a waste of time.' You can feel this start to kick in whenever you get pinned down by someone who seems intent on telling you a very long, boring story when you just need one simple piece of information. It's not long before you start looking for a chance to interrupt and say, 'All very fascinating, I'm sure, but could you just tell me which room the meeting is in?'

Hence the artful composer of clickbait has to walk a fine line: exploit heuristic #1 (get to the good stuff quickly) without getting spotted by heuristic #2 (don't let anyone waste your time).

This gives rise to a sort of 'arms race' between baiter and baited. As we all become more familiar with clickbaiting strategies, we learn to ignore the 'intriguing' headlines that turn out not to be very interesting after all. This spurs the writers to devise more cunning headlines that avoid any tricks and tropes we may have grown weary of, and try to arouse our curiosity in other ways.

The Ongoing Battle

This battle — between advertisers who want to win your attention and your preference not to have your time and attention wasted — is as old as the hills and shows no sign of coming to an end. In fact, it's only going to get worse. The number of commercial websites in the world only ever increases; it never goes down. Hence the pressure mounts on commercial websites to squeeze ever greater returns out of an always increasingly competitive market. As a result, ads and clickbait headlines proliferate and become more and more intrusive.

Once upon a time, on news websites the clickbait headlines were clearly separate from the actual news stories. Today, there are media companies that specialise in placing the clickbait headlines directly in the middle of any news story that features relevant content (e.g. if you're selling anti-wrinkle cream, the clickbait headline gets inserted right into a news story about glamorous celebrities or the latest developments in the cosmetics industry).

The Rise of Reliance

I have pointed out that we all rely on heuristics all the time and we wouldn't be able to function otherwise. It's also true that this reliance is increasing all the time, for one good reason: technology evolves more quickly than we can.

This sometimes shows up in ways that should, perhaps, embarrass us as a species. Back in the 1980s, video cassette recorders were very popular. You could program these devices to record any show you wanted, simply by setting up the clock correctly and then going through a few programming steps. After these machines had been around for a few years, one of the manufacturers conducted a survey. They found that a very high percentage of owners couldn't even set the clock correctly, let alone program the machine to record a TV show. As a species, we could invent a magic machine that could record any TV show; we just weren't very good at learning how to make it do this.

Incidentally, the technology may change but the problems remain the same. These days, the humble video recorder has largely been replaced by its sleeker, smarter digital replacement, the digital video recorder (DVR). These devices can, in theory, be programmed to record TV shows far into the distant future. However, the vast majority are only used to record shows that are on in the next day or so. Why? Because most users can't figure out how to use the more advanced features.

I could cite many other examples of the same phenomenon, and I'm sure you could too. It's not uncommon to see someone struggling with a new piece of technology and, on occasion, being driven to a frenzied rage by a gizmo or gadget that is robustly refusing to do something it is supposed to do very easily. (I have had more bad-tempered fights with my computer printer than I like to admit.)

So the world gets faster, technology seems to progress by leaps and beeps every week, and no one can keep up with all of it, all the time. The result? We have no choice but to rely more on heuristics, on mental shortcuts, than ever before. British philosopher, Alfred North Whitehead recognised this inescapable quality of modern life when he said:

> *"Civilisation advances by extending the number of operations we can perform without thinking about them."*

Group Heuristics: Punks and Panics

It's not just individuals who use heuristics: so do groups and entire societies. At the social level, heuristics give rise to stereotyped thinking. There are many examples of this phenomenon, ranging from the relatively trivial to the serious and worrying.

Whenever a new fashion trend or catchphrase spreads through a community, it's an example of heuristic thinking at the social level — rather than do anything creative (very difficult), people simply adopt ideas that are prevalent among the herd they belong to (much easier). Bertrand Russell once drily observed that:

"Many people would rather die than think; in fact, most do."

Not many people, left to their own devices, would wake up and decide that a 'Mohican' hairstyle, dyed in several clashing colours, would be the perfect way to express their personality. However, during the 'punk rock' era, which was mercifully brief, many young people decided to do this every day (bad news for anyone who had to look at them, but very good news for anyone selling large cans of cheap hairspray).

We also see this when a particular panic story comes along and suddenly spreads through vast swathes of the population. A very good example arose around the turn of the millennium, when people started worrying about a supposed Y2K bug that would affect lots of important computer systems. Countless media headlines suggested we would see bank account reset to zero and planes falling out of the sky as their navigation systems suddenly blanked out. This was utter nonsense from start to finish. The 'bug' was actually just a property of the way Unix systems store dates and related data. It was easily fixed with a line or two of code, and even if it had not been the consequences would have been invisible to most of us.

Watching Witches

To take a more serious example, there have been many instances in history of innocent young women being persecuted for practising 'witchcraft'. At different times and different places, the idea has taken hold that so-called witches are causing problems (making the crops fail or spreading disease) and need to be captured, tortured and killed.

Actually evaluating the evidence, and ascertaining whether anyone is practising witchcraft or whether there's another, entirely more rational reason why something has gone wrong, takes time, effort and a great deal of thought. It's much easier to just go along with 'what everyone knows', and see if hanging a few young women will rectify the situation. Sadly, this kind of entirely tragic stereotyped thinking is still with us, and always will be. It takes many different forms, in many parts of the world, but the fundamental cause is always the same: thoughtful analysis is hard; heuristic and stereotyped thinking is easy.

As a species, it would be great if we could move on from this regrettable tendency to go along with stereotyped thinking, but alas there's little sign we ever will. This doesn't mean we can't try, and I believe we should.

The Sex Pixels

It will come as no surprise that many persuasion games exploit social heuristics and stereotyped thinking. For example, suppose it was your job to try and encourage as many women as possible to buy your fashion and lifestyle magazine. What would you do? Well, you could focus on putting the very best content you could into that magazine — the best reporting, the best photography, the best and most well-written features, and so on. Alternatively, you could just make sure the word 'sex' features on about 45% of all the headlines on the cover.

In 2003, researcher J Sean McCleneghan looked at the front covers of two prominent women's magazines.

> "A purposive sample of all 2001 Cosmopolitan and Glamour magazine front cover issues were content analysed for their respective front cover story titles and subheadings. There were 186 front cover story titles and subheadings studied in the 24 (2001) cover editions. The covers averaged 7.75 individual story titles each and, of course, all the beautiful female cover models wore sensual clothing and make-up. The word 'sex' appeared in more than 45% of the 186 headlines. The word 'sex' was also implied in more than 62% of the headlines (e.g., 'hot love,' 'intimate affairs', 'erotic tastes,' etc.)"

'If it mentions sex it must be interesting' is perhaps the simplest and most obvious instance of stereotyped thinking. By extension, exploiting this rather threadbare heuristic is perhaps the simplest and most obvious strategy a company could adopt. It's certainly hard to imagine that any marketing department using this device has gone through an exhaustive list of strategies before choosing this one. Then again, perhaps we shouldn't be too judgemental. Marketing professionals will tell you they only use the 'sex' strategy because it works — people buy more magazines, more cars, more everything when a way is found to add sex to the equation. In other words, we get the marketing we deserve.

Scent of Success

A lot of the work I do with top companies revolves around heuristics and stereotyped thinking at the social level. In some cases, it's my job to advise on strategies that are likely to work, given what I know about how people 'tick' and what shortcuts can be explored for commercial purposes.

I can't directly discuss examples from my own work since most of it is confidential, but let me give you one example of the sort of thing I mean. This is quite an old example from many years ago. A company was quite proud of its new perfume range, but it wasn't selling as well as they had hoped. The perfume was nice, consumers liked it, the packaging was attractive... it was a great product but retailers reported that it wasn't selling very well. The company called in a consultant who was able to tell them the answer straight away: *put the price up*. Why? Because in this particular market, the prevailing stereotyped thinking was 'expensive = good, cheap = bad'. By pricing their wonderful new scent very competitively, intending to offer 'good value', the company had created the impression that it was a poor-quality product. They changed the strategy, raised the price and won more sales.

Heuristic Shift

Another aspect of my corporate consulting work is about achieving a shift in consumer thinking and perception. In other words, how to work *with* the mechanisms of heuristic, 'shortcut' thinking rather than working *against* them.

My favourite example of this takes the form of an old anecdote that features in several sales and marketing textbooks. It goes like this. There was once a very successful shoe shop. All was going well, but then one day another shoe shop opened just a little way down the street, and put a sign up saying, 'The best shoe shop in this town'. It was quite a bold claim, and they were soon attracting a lot of customers. Not long after, someone opened a *third* shoe shop, and put up a sign saying, 'The best shoe shop in the country'. This was, of course, an even bolder claim, and it wasn't long before they were attracting a lot of attention and trade. Well, the story goes that then a fourth shoe shop opened, and not to be outdone they put up a sign saying, 'The best shoe shop in the world'. Quite a bold claim! Then yet another shoe shop opened and, determined to trump all the others, put up a sign saying, 'The best shoe shop in the entire universe'. At this point, the owner of the first shoe shop was a bit stumped. He thought he too ought to put up a sign, but he couldn't think of anything to beat 'best shop in the universe'.

How did he solve the problem? How did he achieve a radical shift in perception, based on stereotypical thinking? He simply put up a sign saying, 'The best shoe shop on this street'.

This is just an old story that has featured in marketing lectures for decades. However, as well as being quite an amusing tale, it does illustrate an important point. One mode of socially stereotyped thinking is, 'bigger is better'. This is what the shoe shops, with their ever more grandiose signs, were trying to exploit. However, a completely different mode of stereotyped thinking is, 'local = convenient = good'. By asserting that his shop was 'the best on this street', the first shop owner suddenly made his place seem like the one to go to, and all the claims about town / country / universe were made to seem rather irrelevant by comparison.

Discounts That Don't Count

Another delightful example of socially stereotyped thinking involved an car tyre company. In an effort to drum up a bit of business, they mailed out hundreds of discount coupons. However, due to an innocent printing error, some of the coupons offered no savings whatsoever. Surprisingly, the response to these misprinted coupons was just as good as it was to the genuine coupons. Customers who looked at them just saw something that had the look and feel of hundreds of other discount coupons, and so they just *assumed* they offered some sort of discount.

Clothing stores often exploit this tendency we all have to make rather rash assumptions. For example, they often offer discounts or promotional schemes that look very appealing at first glance, despite the fact you have to spend more money than you originally would have done before you obtain any meaningful 'saving'.

Future Heuristics

Heuristics and stereotyped thinking don't just apply to immediate responses and decisions. They also shape people's expectations regarding probabilities, hypothetical situations and future events.

There is an excellent illustration of this in Kevin Dutton's book *Flipnosis*. Suppose I tell you that someone is more than two metres tall. Do you think he is more likely to be a banker or a basketball player?

Given this individual's remarkable height, you probably think he's more likely to play basketball for a living than to work in a bank. If you came to this conclusion, you're in good company: 78% of first-year undergraduates at Cambridge University gave this answer. Unfortunately, it's incorrect.

There are far more bankers in the world than professional basketball players. Just to illustrate the point, let's imagine a world in which there are 100 professional basketball players and 5,000 bankers. How many basketball players are more than two meters tall? Probably quite a lot — let's say 80% (hence 80 in total). How many bankers are more than two meters tall? Probably not that many — let's go with a very conservative estimate of 2% (hence 100 in total). One-hundred is a lot more 80, so our unknown individual is more likely to work in a bank than on a basketball court.

This example, and many others like it, illustrates how easy it is for thinking 'shortcuts' to lead to the wrong conclusion. We can only wonder how often we employ similar shortcuts, and reach similarly wrong conclusions, in business, in relationships and in other areas of everyday life. The good news is that the more aware you are of these kinds of shortcuts, and the errors they can lead to, the less likely you are to make these kinds of mistakes.

Abusing Cues

One other aspect of heuristic thinking takes us into rather worrying territory, especially if you care about the due process of law. The fact that we tend to use mental 'shortcuts' wherever we can has a rather interesting side effect: over-reliance on isolated fragments of evidence. It is perfectly possible for people who have based their views on a single cue or piece of evidence to feel that their conclusions are just as valid as someone who has taken the time and trouble to study *all* the evidence.

As you might expect, this phenomenon is intensified whenever people feel they lack the time, energy or resources to undertake a thorough analysis of a situation. They fasten upon one piece of evidence, come to a conclusion and stick to it.

Slightly less obviously, when people feel rushed, stressed, uncertain, distracted or fatigued, they tend to do the same thing: lock on to one piece of data or evidence and ignore everything else — including other facts that might actually prove far more illuminating.

A Desire for Simplicity

In some respects, this is an understandable tendency: handling one piece of data, and coming to one (rather rushed) conclusion, is massively easier than actually examining complex matters in detail and assessing many fine nuances of conflicting data.

Unfortunately, it can lead to some flawed projections and expectations. In my own work, I notice this particularly with regard to the art and science of body language, which is one part of non-verbal communication or NVC. I meet lots of people who would like to understand more about body language, and it's a subject that I teach very often. In fact, I'm pleased to say it has become one of my best-selling talks and masterclasses, and I can understand why — being able to read someone like a book is a very useful skill. Although I love this subject, one problem crops up time and again: students want it to be simpler than it really is.

Studying body language seriously is not as simple as saying 'this gesture has this specific meaning'. Instead, a trained body language expert tends to look for *clusters* of data which *considered together* can reveal quite a lot about someone's thoughts, feelings and intentions. For example, one might say that a particular stance, combined with a specific gesture and a specific vocal inflection, tends to indicate insincerity. Take any one of these elements out of the picture, and the conclusion becomes correspondingly less reliable.

I've met many students who don't want to accept that this is the case. They want it to be a case of 'this one gesture means this one thing'. While I may want to teach them about body language, I don't like having to be the one to explain that the subject is not quite as simple as they want it to be. This is the 'one piece of evidence' heuristic in action. It is not easy to overcome.

Feeling Bad

So far, we've looked at the way heuristics and stereotypical thinking can lead to the wrong conclusion in a purely rational sense. However, they can also lead us to inappropriate *feelings* and *emotional* responses.

Consider this example. Imagine you have some tickets for a raffle and the winning number is 452. Would you feel more hard-done by if you were holding ticket number 451 or number 183? Most people would feel they just narrowly missed out if they had number 451, whereas in reality each ticket has exactly the same chance of winning.

Several advertising strategies rely on evoking an emotional response that is not really warranted, or at least lacks authentic foundations. To take a fairly obvious example, when a record label launches a new album by a star of the music world, they attempt to create feelings of excitement and anticipation, and to engender the 'herd instinct' feeling that everyone else is gearing up to buy the album and there's some merit in buying it as soon as possible. We have all seen this pattern so often that we rarely pause to see how strange it is.

A far better strategy, on every level, would be to wait until the album comes out, wait to see if people think it's any good, read plenty of reviews and *then* decide whether or not to buy it. This would greatly reduce the risk of purchasing junk and wasting money.

It's also interesting to note what happens after the promotional budget has been exhausted — the exact same album, which a few weeks ago was apparently a vital, unmissable, must-have part of everyone's listening pleasure, is now just another old product, and the promotional circus has moved to another album, another artist, another attempt to coat the mundane in the golden gloop of painted-on importance.

Scare Stories

The same strategy is apparent when you book a hotel room or an airline ticket online — many items are flagged as 'reduced availability'. In some cases, this may be accurate information. Far more commonly, it is just blatant 'scarcity marketing'. The 'very few left' claim suggests that the item is in demand (an emotional appeal to 'herd instinct'), and that a hasty purchase is advisable. It may even lend a tinge of 'excitement' to the proceedings. The happy shopper, upon completing the purchase, feels a sense of victory, of having secured a bargain against the odds and against the clock.

There are two obvious observations to offer about this practice. The first is that if you get a sense of excitement from buying a hotel room, you could perhaps consider recalibrating what you consider 'exciting' in life. There are people who parachute into volcanoes for fun.

Secondly, sift as you may the accumulated evidence of human commerce, you will never find an instance where 'buying on impulse or under time pressure' works out to be a better strategy than 'take your time, give it some thought and be wary of sharp practices'. Yet 'scarcity marketing' will always be with us, simply because it works.

Heuristics of the Psychic

So far in this chapter I have mentioned a few ways in which some people can exploit heuristic thinking for their own ends, such as persuading the rest of us to buy things that aren't really worth buying. What is perhaps even more fascinating is that heuristic thinking can lead someone to come to false conclusions *about themselves*.

I have already made it clear that in this book I am not concerned with the issue of whether or not psychic powers are real. There's no need to rehash a debate that has been going on since ancient times, never goes anywhere and never will.

Instead, let's talk about something more interesting. Let us just assume, for the sake of discussion, that while there may be some genuine psychics, there are also some people who offer psychic readings and related services even though they are about as psychic as a plant pot. The curious thing is that they may be sincerely convinced they *do* have psychic abilities — purely as a result of heuristic thinking.

The Delusion Dungeon

It works like this. Anne starts messing about with tarot cards just for fun, and she gives little three minute 'readings' for friends just for a laugh. It's nothing but a harmless pastime, a little bit of informal fun between friends that makes a nice change from watching TV. Anne makes lots of statements and serves up plenty of wild guesses and speculation about the future.

Over the next days and weeks, if *anything* happens that seems to correspond with *anything* Anne said, even if it requires a little 'interpretation' to fit, Anne's friend will tell her that she turned out to be remarkably accurate. It isn't true: Anne's hit rate may be just one lucky guess out of a hundred, and no better than the humble laws of probability would allow. However, if it happens even once or twice, Anne might well start to feel that maybe she does, after all, have some sort of special gift. This, in turn, encourages her to give more readings.

As she gives more readings, she is constantly learning what sort of statements and predictions tend to win subsequent validation, and hence getting better at saying things that 'come true'. Thus the cycle is completed: more readings give rise to more amazed reports of peerless accuracy, which beget more readings. This wheel does not have to turn many times before Anne starts to believe she is a bona fide psychic, benevolently sharing her insights with the world. She may carry on giving readings for free, or she may feel that her talents are worthy of a modest fee. At this point, she will make the happy discovery that the number of people willing to pay for a reading knows no limit.

Constructing the Fable

It is interesting to look at the number of emotional drivers involved in this scenario. To actually tally all of Anne's guesses, and correctly assess how many turned out wrong (nearly all) and how many were slightly correct (one or two) would be time-consuming and fairly dull. To notice a correlation between something she said and a later event delivers that satisfying frisson of surprise and amazement; it takes us out of the humdrum, everyday world and into the realm of strange powers, unseen forces and exciting potential: what if we could all learn to foretell the future? *Wouldn't that be cool!*

Hence there is a strong emotional current leading people to the 'Hey, wow! Something magical happened!' response, rather than the 'One or two lucky guesses — so what?' response.

Next, think about it from the point of view of Anne's friends. Which of these sounds more interesting and appealing to you:

(a) I have a friend who looks at cards, waffles on a bit, makes wild guesses and now and again gets a few things right by chance; or

(b) I have a friend who has remarkably accurate powers of precognition, and is apparently able to transcend the veil of time.

I'm pretty sure all but the most stone-cold-hearted of people would prefer option (b). Everyone wants to be friends with someone with amazing talents and super powers.

Finally, look at it from Anne's point of view. She didn't set out to be deceptive or manipulative. She hasn't a trace of malice or trickery in her body, and she was merely having fun. Yet her friends, unprompted and unbidden, keep telling her that she has the gift of prophecy, and they have no apparent reason to lie about this.

What's she going to do? It would take remarkable intellectual detachment to see the whole picture, and to understand that she is not, in fact, glimpsing the future. We all want to feel special, talented and gifted, and it is far more seductive and alluring to accept, in a suitably humble spirit, that we have been chosen by the universe to serve as a precious, important portal for pinpoint predictions that can help people to live better lives.

That human beings are prone to delusions about their own abilities is not news. We see evidence of this all the time on televised talent shows, where legions of young hopefuls arrive prepared to enjoy a career on a par with the greatest singers in history, sincerely unaware that they can sing no better than a particularly tone-deaf walrus. This truth will also be familiar to office workers blessed with one of those managers who is, in his own mind, a captain of industry and a prince among men, whereas everyone else in the office regards him as a pitiful, shambling shrine to negative achievement and poor personal hygiene.

What's particularly interesting about the example of Anne the psychic superstar is not just the delusion itself, but all the feedback mechanisms that create and sustain the delusion. Both the 'psychic' and her clients are prey to heuristics that work well in one sense (providing a sense of wonder, intrigue, fascination and so on) but very badly in another (ascribing to Anne a talent or ability she does not possess).

In one context, this may be trivial and lead to no harm. If Anne and her friends want to believe she sometimes glimpses the future, well, where's the harm? In other contexts, the consequences can be more grave. Many so-called 'healers' believe they have the gift of healing for precisely the same reasons that Anne, in my example, came to think she had the gift of prophecy. If such a 'healer' tells a cancer sufferer to abandon medical treatment and rely on their own healing ability — which has actually happened — the consequences can be dire. It is not going too far to say that in some cases, a simple awareness of heuristic thinking, and the errors to which it can give rise, can save lives.

The Psychic Who Wasn't

My example of Anne the psychic superstar, and how she comes to believe in her impressive yet sadly fictional talent, is not just a made-up story I plucked out of thin air. This kind of thing really happens. For fairly obvious reasons, it is not often documented. As I mentioned, not many have the intellectual detachment and perspective necessary to see what's really going on, and even fewer will have the ability to write about the experience in an interesting way. The best example I know of is found in a book by British parapsychologist Susan Blackmore. In her excellent book, *Adventures of a Parapsychologist*, she tells the story of how her younger self gradually came to believe that she had some sort of psychic ability. She didn't set out to fool herself or anyone else, and she had no cunning plan to make a name for herself in the psychic world. She just started giving readings for fun and received what seemed like numerous sincere and convincing reports of how accurate her words had turned out to be. Only later, after a lot of thought and a more systematic review of her own 'performance', did the truth dawn upon her.

Cambridge psychologist Nicholas Humphrey, in his book *The Inner Eye*, is also very eloquent on this subject, and has postulated a range of mechanisms by which someone might arrive at the conclusion they are psychic despite having *no desire to do so* and no intention of making any such claim. He goes further, and explains how even someone caught cheating or fabricating results could remain unaware they are being deceptive or doing anything wrong.

M Lamar Keene, in his book *The Psychic Mafia*, refers to sincere people who have managed to delude themselves about their psychic ability as 'shut-eyes'. They don't actually have any paranormal ability but are, without being aware of it, fooling themselves and others.

Gilan's Persuasion Tips

Here are three simple tips for you based on this chapter:

- Look out for the heuristics that are involved in persuasion games all the time, and especially the ones that affect you or the people you deal with.

- Use heuristic shift to your advantage: remember that 'best on this street' can sometimes beat 'best in the universe'.

- Trying to sway someone's judgement is one thing, but it's often more effective to let them sway their *own* judgement (with just a few subtle nudges from you).

Summary

In this chapter, we looked at the mental shortcuts known as heuristics. They are useful, but can also be seriously misleading. Individuals use heuristics, but so do groups and entire societies, which can lead to socially stereotyped thinking. Heuristics can affect immediate response or future expectations. They can affect not just rational processes (leading to errors of judgement) but also inappropriate feelings and emotions. Heuristics can also lead people to unwittingly delude themselves.

Persuaders exploit heuristics in ways both subtle and superficial. Slapping the word 'sex' on a magazine cover isn't clever, but it does work. Figuring out how to achieve a subtle heuristic shift in attitudes, within a given market or demographic, is more difficult — but it can be done.

You would think that if you know about heuristics, you can avoid the thinking errors they often lead to. Alas, this is not always the case. The problem is, you don't just have one mind — you have *two*. And one of them is going to fall for the tricks, snares and delusions every time. This is the subject of the next chapter.

(At the very start of this book I invited you to look at the NITE photo. You may still be wondering why I claim you did *not* see what you *think* you saw. We will get to this fairly soon. I haven't forgotten!)

5: Systems 1 and 2

"Thaw with her gentle persuasion is more powerful than Thor with his hammer. The one melts, the other breaks into pieces."

— Henry David Thoreau

Flash of Inspiration

What's 45 x 45?

Can you solve it in your head?

I expect most of you looked at this problem and had little trouble coming to the conclusion that you don't know the answer, you certainly can't work it out in your head and you don't care. This is the normal reaction from everyone except mathematical prodigies and human/robot hybrids with eerie metallic faces.

Strange as it may seem, you *do* know the answer and you *can* work it out in your head — even if you think you have the mathematical aptitude of a mollusc. I'll prove this to you before the end of this chapter and turn you into a mathematical genius.

The point is that there is a handy 'shortcut' that can transform what seems to be a tough problem to solve in your head into a very easy one. If you think about this maths problem the traditional way that you were taught in school, it seems like an awful lot of hard work to do in your head. That's the long, slow way of going about it. On the other hand, when you use the mental shortcut that I'll explain later, the answer flashes into your mind almost instantly. That's the fast way of thinking about it.

All of which is by way of introduction to the theme of this chapter, which is the difference between fast and slow thinking. We have already established that one mode of thinking ('take your time, be careful, use plenty of processing power') can combat some common thinking errors (false assumptions, skewed emotional response, delusional perceptions). It should therefore come as no surprise when I tell you that we have two different speeds or 'systems' of thinking: slow and fast. In fact, you use both systems every day. They are both active all the time, but one can predominate over the other.

Hare and Tortoise

You may remember Aesop's classic fable of *The Hare and The Tortoise* having a race. The Hare was a very fast runner, but made the assumption that he would win no matter what and actually ended up losing. The Tortoise was slow yet wise and eventually won the race. Useful as this metaphor is, it only touches the surface of the many wonderful differences between slow and fast thinking — both of which have their uses and their perils.

I started this chapter with an arithmetic problem, which is quite possibly the worst way to start any chapter that's not in a textbook. If you asked everyone you know to list their favourite ways to pass the time, 'doing mental arithmetic' wouldn't even make the Top 100. This being the case, surely the only thing worse that sticking a maths problem in this chapter would be to add another one. This is exactly what I'm going to do now, but please stay with me and don't flip the page. *I promise this gets interesting*:

What's 14 x 37?

I expect your reply will be pretty much the same as before: don't know, don't care.

That's okay, but now let me put it another way. What's 14 x 37 *most likely* to be?

- about 32

- about 500

- about 650,000

I expect you feel, quite strongly, that the second answer is more likely to be correct — and you're absolutely right (it's actually 519). What's *fun* and *fascinating* about this is that you have an innate sense of what would be a plausible answer to the problem, even if at the same time you are sure you couldn't work it out in your head. You know that you don't know the answer, but you have a feeling about what it ought to be.

Where this gets interesting is to ask yourself how often you apply these different kinds of 'fast' and 'slow' thinking every day without even realising it.

Here's another example. Take a look at this photo.

As soon as you see this photo you decide the man is angry without giving it any conscious thought. Your mind responds in automatic mode and you apply intuitive thinking. Furthermore, your assessment extends into the future — you expect he is about to say some very unkind words, probably in a loud and strident voice.

Two Systems

These two modes of thinking have been studied for decades. Psychologists Keith Stanovich and Richard West label them System 1 and System 2, thereby demonstrating that if you want people to name things in fun and interesting ways, don't ask research psychologists.

Let's look at the difference between the two. (Most of what follows is a summary of ideas presented in Daniel Kahneman's justly celebrated book, *Thinking, Fast and Slow*. If you want further details, that's the book to go to and I highly recommend it.)

We can characterise System 1 as 'fast thinking'. This kind of thinking occurs rapidly and with little conscious effort or sense of will.

Here are some examples of System 1 in action:

- Noticing one object is larger than another.

- Turning towards a sudden sound or a noise you weren't expecting.

- Completing the phrase 'Salt and...'.

- Responding with a look of disgust when someone shows you a picture you find horrible or repulsive.

- Figuring out 3 + 1.

We can characterise System 2 as 'slow' thinking. This kind of thinking takes longer and involves knowing, intentional effort, most commonly towards solving a problem or performing some sort of calculation or assessment. When you use System 2 thinking you have a sense of personally achieving something, being mentally focused and making what you think are intelligent choices and decisions. Concentration is a feature of System 2 thinking, and if someone or something distracts you then you get that familiar feeling of annoyance at the disruption. Here are some examples of System 2 in action:

- Sorting items into two or more sets (for example taking a deck of cards and separating reds and blacks, or the four different suits).

- Making the effort to listen to one particular person's voice in a crowded situation.

- In social or formal situations, trying to make sure you observe the correct protocol or ensure you behave in a respectful and appropriate way.

- Giving someone a set of directions or instructions that have to be followed in a specific way.

- Looking over a logical argument or calculation to see if you think it's correct and free from errors.

It is interesting to look at how these two systems of thinking work together.

System 1 is automatic, whereas System 2 involves at least a modest amount of effort (although in normal circumstances you only use a small percentage of your total capacity).

System 1 is constantly offering data to System 2, in the form of impressions and feelings. When System 2 endorses them, these impressions become formed into beliefs, and impulses become shaped into voluntary actions. On those occasions when all of this happens smoothly, System 2 adopts the data from System 1 with hardly any modification, so you are barely even aware that this has happened.

When System 1 encounters a problem, it asks System 2 for detailed analysis to solve the difficulty. In other words, System 2 is triggered when System 1 can't handle a question or a problem satisfactorily.

The Fun of 1

System 1 thinking is remarkable, and can even save your life in the face of sudden threats or danger. The fact that we can do so many things on an instinctive or 'automatic' level is a tribute to the wonderful complexities and richness of the human brain, and the way it has evolved. However, as we have seen, it is prone to errors of judgement and doesn't always lead us to the correct conclusion.

For precisely this reason, expert persuaders often make it their business to try to engage with your System 1 thinking rather than System 2. Loosely expressed, it presents a 'soft target', or at least a softer one than System 2 thinking.

Consider a TV commercial for a new car. The car itself is shown in pristine, immaculate, showroom condition. It is driven by a confident, relaxed, attractive man or woman (depending on who the advert is aimed at). The car is shown being driven along an empty road, in a beautiful scenic location. There is music playing, intended to convey excitement, happiness or importance. Every single shot makes the car look beautiful — a gleaming, superbly designed example of engineering excellence. The advertisers may even try to suggest that the car comes with sexual magnetism as a standard feature.

It's easy to see all the System 1 triggers involved here: attractive visuals, appealing music, positive aspiration, shiny happy people, quality, excellence, an easy life in beautiful places, sex. Of course, System 2 thinking recognises that literally *nothing* in the advert has anything to do with the merits or otherwise of buying this particular car. It may be a very good car, or it may be an overpriced lump of badly made rubbish that will break down with monotonous and expensive regularity. You won't be driving it along empty roads in exotic locations — you'll be stuck in traffic with everyone else, swearing under your breath at how late you're going to be. Nor will the car have a remarkably positive effect on your romantic life. There are many things in this world that may help you find the partner of your dreams, but an efficient fuel injection system isn't one of them — or shouldn't be.

System 1 and Cold Reading

You won't be surprised to hear that my friends in the psychic industry know it is in their interests to appeal to System 1 thinking rather than System 2. When giving someone a personal reading, they keep everything easy to understand and respond to, and also offer whatever emotional comfort the client happens to want.

If the client wants to hear that despite some recent troubles everything is going to work out just fine in the end, that's what the psychic sees indicated in the cards. This strategy tends to generate good repeat business and referrals. The alternative would be to say things such as, 'Things have been pretty bad lately and guess what… they're going to get a whole lot worse. I can't say exactly how bad things are going to get, but let's put it this way: don't start reading any long books.' Psychics who offer this kind of outlook tend not to stay in business for very long, no matter how profound their psychic gifts may be.

However, the ways in which cold readers snare us in the coils of our own System 1 thinking can be very subtle. Consider a fairly typical piece of psychic spiel such as this:

> *"There's an indication here of some concern over a health issue, and this may be to do with you or someone you've been thinking of. The signs are that there's going to be a positive outcome, so no need to worry, but tell me — is this you, or someone that's been in your thoughts?"*

Note that there is nothing here to trigger System 2 analysis, and no real opportunity for System 2 to come into play. If it did, the client might well start analysing what's going on and asking unhelpful questions: how can gazing at some tarot cards possibly convey meaningful information about my friends and their health? And if I'm paying you to be psychic, why are you asking me questions?

Instead, the client is offered a simple question and two options: is this about you, or someone else? (Note that these two options neatly encapsulate every possibility in the universe) As soon as the client even begins to respond to this, he or she has been lured down the alley of

System 1 thinking, and is likely to say something about either their own health or that of someone they know. The odds are stacked in the psychic's favour, given that few of us live in an idyllic medical paradise where everyone strides around enjoying robust, vigorous good health at all times.

What happens in those rare cases where the client has not, in fact, been thinking of any issues at all related to health? Does the psychic admit she's wrong and has been making it all up? Not quite. Psychics are no more prone to do this than rain is prone to fall upwards. The standard response is:

> *"Ah, well if it hasn't happened yet then it'll be coming up soon, so will you watch out for that? But remember, please don't worry, the signs are that it'll clear up and the outcome will be very positive."*

Cognitive Distractions

System 2 thinking can often save us from the errors and delusions associated with System 1 thinking. One might say that System 2 should put System 1 in its place — just like the Tortoise put the Hare in his place. However, there are many times when System 2 fails to do this. This failure can usually be attributed to one of two factors: cognitive distractions and cognitive illusions. These happen to be two of my favourite subjects for one very good reason: they have helped me to earn a living for the past ten years or so.

Cognitive illusions are quite a big subject, so I'll keep those for the next chapter. For now, let's just take a look at cognitive distractions.

The Cognitive Model

There are many branches of psychology that fascinate me, but none more than the wonderful and intriguing realm of *cognitive* psychology. This deals with perception and the thought processes by which we build a mental model of the world and try to figure out the best way to interact with it. You are probably a student of cognitive psychology whether you realise it or not. If you have ever mistaken a stranger for someone you know, and wondered why, then you've been interested in cognitive psychology. Likewise, if you've ever felt you had a very good memory of something, and then seen it again and wondered why your recollection was way off the mark (the so-called 'false memory' syndrome) then you've been interested in cognitive psychology.

So, what's cognitive distraction all about? As we have already seen, System 2 thinking requires attention and concentration. If sufficient distraction comes along, System 2 thinking becomes impaired and can start to fail. The most startling and popular demonstration of this in recent times was a video created by researchers Christopher Chabris and Daniel Simons. The video is discussed in their remarkable book *The Invisible Gorilla*. (If you haven't yet seen this video, you can find it on the Internet if you search for 'Selective Attention Test' or 'Did You Spot The Gorilla'.)

The video shows two teams passing basketballs between them. Viewers are invited to focus on just one team and count the number of passes they make. Most viewers have little trouble correctly counting the number of passes made — but in doing so, they completely miss the fact that during the video a man in a gorilla suit walked into the frame, beat his chest for the camera, and then walked out again.

It seems unbelievable that anyone could fail to spot a rather large, hairy gorilla walking into what is, after all, a very simple video that takes place in a confined space with no background distractions. What it proves is a remarkable flaw in System 2 thinking: when most or all of our System 2 resources are aimed towards one task, we tend to ignore or not be aware of other tasks and other data (such as the presence of a large ape).

This doesn't matter a great deal when you're watching an academic research video created expressly for the purpose of making you miss a gorilla. However, in other circumstances it matters a great deal. To take one obvious example, if you are distracted while driving, you may well fail to notice another car or a smaller item in your field of vision such as a cyclist or a child.

System Overload

When psychologists describe these limitations, they refer to cognitive resources and cognitive load. In simple terms, you have a finite amount of mental processing power available for System 2 thinking. If you are preoccupied with a task that requires all or nearly all of your System 2 resources, you have none to spare for other tasks.

Here are two simple demonstrations that make this clear.

Look at the first picture and try to find the bold **2**. Then look at the second picture and find the bold **2** again.

(Graphic reproduced from 2025 Research Paradigms)

It took longer with the second picture because solving the problem required more of your mental resources. In the first picture, your brain only had to make a selection based on contrast. In the second picture it had to make a selection based on both contrast and shape.

Here's a second example that I think you'll find a little more fascinating and, to be honest, a bit more annoying. Turn to the section of colour images on page 93 of this book. Look at the graphic entitled 'The Stroop Test'. All you have to do is say which colour each word is printed in (as opposed to just reading each word). You will probably find this hard because of the cognitive load involved.

When I started playing chess, I learned an offensive tactic known as a 'pin'. Pinning my opponent's piece means that he can't move it, because if he does one of my own pieces will place his king in check. In other words, his piece is rendered inactive until he undoes the pin by moving his king somewhere safe. While my opponent's piece is pinned, I can use my other pieces to launch an attack.

It's the same when you are experiencing cognitive load: your cognitive resources are 'pinned' and can't be used for very much, if anything. This explains how you sometimes miss what might be vital or seemingly obvious pieces of information, or how someone is able to bypass your critical faculties and place influential ideas or messages into your mind.

Exploiting the Limits

Persuaders can exploit both cognitive distraction and cognitive overload. If I am trying to sell you a new computer, I can draw your attention to lots of things about it, including how nice it looks, the very detailed and impressive technical specifications, the fact that lots of people are buying this same model, and my excellent after-sales service. All this information provides plenty of cognitive distraction, especially if I'm good at selling and know how to keep the presentation flowing and amicable. I might even add a few good jokes plus a little bit of flattery ("I wouldn't recommend this for everyone, but someone who does a lot of important work like you really needs a high-spec machine you can rely on.")

This distraction may be sufficient to override your slow System 2 thinking so you don't notice that (a) you can get exactly the same machine, and the same deal, 50% cheaper from the next supplier, and (b) I'm a convicted fraudster and my name and photo are all over consumer advice websites saying 'Do not buy from this man'.

It's not uncommon for people who are trying to sell things to use a lot of dazzle and spectacle: loud, pounding music, flashing and strafing lights, dry ice, sexy young people running around athletically handing out glossy flyers, and so on. If ever you encounter this kind of thing, you may want to consider the remote possibility that someone is trying to distract part of your mind. Specifically, the System 2 part that might ask awkward questions like, 'Yes, but is this product actually any good? And if it is, why do you need all this razzle-dazzle to sell it?'

Override Denied

As we have seen, System 1 thinking is triggered by those situations where a rapid or even an instinctive, automatic reaction is required, such as reacting to a sudden noise or flash of light and trying to ascertain whether we or not we are in danger.

We can all consciously override our System 1 thinking to some extent — which is why people can train themselves to remain calm and methodical in dangerous situations (e.g. firefighters and lion tamers). However, we only have a limited ability to do this. There is often a conflict between the automatic System 1 reaction and our conscious will to override it with our more rational System 2 faculties.

This ability varies from one individual to another. Some people can get their System 2 thinking to prevail quite well, others find it a bit of a challenge and some never learn to do it at all. In my stage work as a mentalist, I often have to read people and gauge what sort of thinking — System 1 or System 2 — I am dealing with. When I have someone up on stage with me, I have to ask myself if I can trigger an automatic, unthinking System 1 response, or whether I should appeal to that person's more rational System 2 thinking patterns. When I get it right, I can usually elicit the response I want. When I don't… well, let's not talk about *those* shows!

The Psychic Snare

It will be obvious that skilled cold readers generally want clients to use System 1 thinking so that, for example, they will respond to emotional cues and not ask too many analytical questions.

I sometimes hear it said that cold readers don't like clients asking too many questions. This isn't quite correct. A cold reader *welcomes* questions so long as they are consistent with the supposedly psychic consultation taking place. If the client asks, 'What can you see about my romantic life?', or 'Are there good indications on the career front?', the cold reader is perfectly happy. These questions show that the client has bought into the psychic scenario, in a way that can perhaps generously be described as 'uncritical', and is focused on emotional concerns. In other words, these are questions arising from System 1 thinking. Psychics are happy about these kinds of questions since they provide them with a career.

The kinds of questions that cold readers tend not to love quite so much are those that arise from System 2 thinking. Here's an example: 'How could gazing at the palm of my hand possibly reveal anything about the romantic encounters I may have in the near future? Please explain this, unless you want to accept that this is a time-wasting farce.'

This kind of System 2 question is rather fatal to the psychic scenario and is not, in my experience, warmly welcomed by those who walk among us burdened with the power of deep psychic insight.

Given that cold readers prefer clients to use System 1 thinking, how do they encourage this? In some cases, it can be very simple. Skilled cold readers are good at keeping their readings easy to understand and easy to appreciate. They speak clearly and couch everything in informal, chatty language that anyone can relate to, often using familiar figures of speech. This isn't as easy as it sounds. We have all seen people who are terrible at explaining even quite simple ideas. There are bad, mumbling teachers whose 'lessons' are worse than no teaching at all, and dull executives who can turn any corporate presentation into a snore-a-thon you'd eat your own foot to get out of.

In contrast, the skilled cold reader can deliver a smooth, improvised, twenty-minute reading that is always clear, always easy to listen to and always expressed in terms the client can relate to. This is a skill to be admired, especially by anyone interested in persuasion games.

Time to Rhyme

It's not just cold readers who want to keep things simple and easy to understand. There are many people who have to wrestle with the challenge of achieving clear, simple and effective communication. When I work with marketing and advertising agencies, it's my job to share some of the things I know about the mind and how it works so that they can devise successful campaigns.

A very good example, which I often discuss at length, is the slogan, 'Coke Adds Life'. Trust me, it takes a lot of smart people a lot of time, effort and research to come up with a slogan as good and effective as that. You may think, 'But it's just three words, anyone could have made that up'. I beg to differ. Finding a slogan that simplifies the brand's appeal to just three words, and that will work as part of an integrated and well-focused ad campaign, is a seriously difficult challenge. Achieving simplicity is a very complicated business!

One advertising technique that we're all familiar with is the advertising jingle or slogan that rhymes. 'A Mars a day helps you work, rest and play' / 'Don't just book it, Thomas Cook it' / 'If your drain is being naughty, call triple four forty forty'.

There's a little more to this than you might realise. Clearly, rhymes make things easier to remember, and a really good or clever rhyme can become an 'ear-worm' — something you can't get out of your mind even if you want to.

However, that's not the only reason for using slogans that rhyme. Matthew McGlone conducted a study which he rather brilliantly entitled, 'Birds of a feather flock conjointly'. He created pairs of aphorisms that said much the same thing, the only difference being that one set rhymed and the other did not, like this:

'Woes unite Foes' / 'Woes unite Enemies'
'A fault confessed is half redressed' / 'A fault admitted is half redressed'

He presented these pithy sayings to students and asked them to rate how insightful they were, the only difference being that some students saw the rhyming versions and some saw the non-rhyming ones. The aphorisms that rhymed scored more highly than the ones that did not.

Rhymes don't just make lines more memorable — they also convey a sense of insight, truth, value, authority and so on. It's interesting to speculate about why this might be so. Before the advent of widespread literacy, a lot of tribal information was passed down orally from each generation to the next. Mnemonic techniques were used to try to preserve the integrity of the information handed down, with rhyme being one of them. Even today, many traditional sayings and proverbs incorporate rhyme. Maybe when we hear rhymes, we associate them with proverbs and wisdom handed down through the ages.

At this point, I'd just like to mention that a lot of my work involves helping companies and organisations to understand how to be persuasive, so they sell more and make more money. Remember:

When you need an expert persuasion plan
Hire Gilan — he is The Man!

Maths Genius

At the start of this chapter, I promised to turn you into a maths genius. Here we go.

Let's start with this: what's 25 x 25? Here's the shortcut:

- look at the first digit (2)
- multiply this by itself plus 1 (so 2 x 3, which = 6)
- stick 25 on the end

And... we're done! 25 x 25 = 625.

This works for any two-digit number ending in 5. I'll do another one for you. What's 65 x 65?

- look at the first digit (6)
- multiply this by itself plus 1 (so 6 x 7, which = 42)
- stick 25 on the end

Hence we get 4,225, which is the correct answer.

Now then, what's 45 x 45?

I expect you got the answer right. (Check with a calculator if you want, or turn back a few pages to the 'Find the bold 2' puzzle and look at the fake caption underneath it.)

See, I *knew* you could do it! You are now officially a mathematical genius!

Gilan's Persuasion Tips

Here are three simple tips for you based on this chapter:

- When you want to persuade, do what you can to encourage System 1 thinking.

- Cognitive distraction is your friend: it can keep System 2 thinking from coming into play, or neutralise it.

- A lot of your persuasion success will come down to your ability to keep things easy to follow and easy to understand. This is a lot more difficult than it sounds.

When you need an expert persuasion plan
Hire Gilan — he is The Man!

Summary

In this chapter, we looked at System 1 thinking (fast, impulsive, uncritical) and System 2 thinking (thoughtful, rational, slow). They both have their uses, and you use both all the time, as and when appropriate. There's nothing wrong with this, but the unthinking, uncritical aspect of System 1 thinking can lead to problems.

Persuaders generally want to encourage System 1 thinking because that makes their life a lot easier. There are many ways to do this, such as cognitive distractions. Another has to do with the art of keeping things simple: easy to follow, easy to understand, easy to absorb. This is a lot harder than it looks, but good advertisers and psychics make it look easy.

I said that System 2 thinking sometimes fails to come into play when it should. Two common causes are cognitive distractions and cognitive illusions. We've looked at cognitive distractions, but cognitive illusions are such a big subject that I've left them for the next chapter. It all starts with two lines, and two tables...

6: Cognitive Illusions

"People almost invariably arrive at their beliefs not on the basis of proof but on the basis of what they find attractive."

— *Blaise Pascal*

Illusion Confusion

In the previous chapter, I explained that System 2 thinking can sometimes fail to override System 1 thinking, even in situations where this would be advantageous. One reason this can happen is cognitive distraction, which we've just had a look at. The other is cognitive illusion.

Suppose I ask you to look at these two table tops (ignore the table legs). They are clearly slightly different shapes and sizes… but which one has the largest surface area? The dark one on the left, or the lighter one on the right?

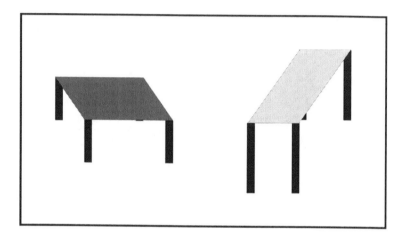

In fact the two table tops are absolutely identical in size and shape — only the shading is different. You can check if you don't believe me!

Once you have actually verified the facts, your System 2 thinking gets updated and you *understand* that the two grey tabletops are identical in size and shape, even though you still *see* them as different.

This goes to show that there are some contexts in which you need to disregard your immediate or most obvious perception and let your System 2 thinking prevail. This can be very hard to do. Whenever a witness asserts rather adamantly, 'I know what I saw with my own eyes', it can be difficult for them to understand that what they saw isn't necessarily real.

Visual illusions of this nature serve as a good metaphor for *cognitive* illusions. Just as your eyes can be fooled by visual tricks like these, your mind and your perception of the word can be fooled by cognitive illusions.

Illusions of Mind

It's fair to say that cognitive illusions can be more stubborn than visual ones. When you first saw the two tables optical illusion, you probably thought the two shaded areas were different in size and shape. Now that you know better, you wouldn't be fooled by it again. Although you still *see* the same illustration of the two tables, you *know* that your first impressions were wrong, and that the two grey areas are identical in size and shape. You have successfully updated your mental model, or cognitive model, of the world around you. People find it *much* harder to do this with cognitive illusions. Even when people know about a cognitive illusion, and are given all the relevant information, the illusion can still persist.

To take a very common example, consider astrology. We know that not a single facet of astrology has any factual or rational basis whatsoever. The positions of the sun, the moon and other heavenly bodies have literally nothing to do with your personality, your potential, your destiny, who you're compatible with or any of the events in your life. We can understand that people may once have thought this was possible, at a much earlier point in human civilisation. However, we now know enough about how the world works to be able to state, as a matter of plain fact, that astrology has no factual basis whatsoever.

Nonetheless, the cognitive illusion that astrology *does* work has proved very persistent among its practitioners, students and fans. Let me be clear: I am not suggesting for one second that anyone who believes astrology works is stupid or unintelligent. They are simply prey to an enduring cognitive illusion, and that's all. This wouldn't be of much concern to the rest of us, if it were not for the fact that we might occasionally be affected by someone else's belief in the subject. Some people have been known to use astrology for recruitment decisions. How frustrating it must be if you are very well qualified for a particular job, and willing to work hard, but you never get the chance simply because you're Aries and they were looking for a Capricorn?

The Persistence of Myth

I find it remarkable that someone can understand what cognitive illusions are, and even understand that one of their own beliefs is a cognitive illusion, and yet still remain firmly snared within its tentacles. To put it the other way around, it is certainly the case that knowing about a cognitive illusion is no defence against it.

Most of us are well aware of simple sales and marketing strategies, such as the 'scarcity marketing' and red flashes saying 'Special discount offer!'. Nonetheless, many of us still fall for them.

One very good example is cold reading. In reading this book, you may feel that my references to how cold reading works might possibly damage the psychic industry. This isn't going to happen. I can promise you that the cold readers of the world won't have the slightest problem with either me or my book for one good reason: it won't have any impact on their work whatsoever.

This is how it should be. I'm not here to upset anyone, debunk anything or put anyone out of business. I only mention cold reading for the reason I gave at the start of this book: cold readers are among the world's finest players of the persuasion game, and I admire them tremendously. When I travelled to England to study with Ian Rowland, I was amazed at his ability to tell me about more or less any aspect of my life in remarkable detail. I knew that it was just cold reading, yet the illusion of real 'psychic insight' was remarkably persistent and effective.

True-Believer Syndrome

In *The Psychic Mafia* by M Lamarr Keene, he mentions people who continued to believe in this or that psychic phenomena even after it was shown to be fake. Keene classified this as a cognitive disorder, and regarded it as a key factor in the success of many psychic mediums. The term 'true believer' was used earlier by Eric Hoffer in his 1951 book to describe the psychological roots of fanatical groups.

Keene tells the story of his partner, a psychic medium named Raoul. Even after Raoul openly admitted that he was a fake, some of their congregation persisted in their belief that he was genuine. Keene wrote, 'I knew how easy it was to make people believe a lie, but I didn't expect the same people, confronted with the lie, would choose it over the truth. No amount of logic can shatter a faith consciously based on a lie.'

The Skeptic's Dictionary provides another example of the same phenomenon. In 1988, at the request of an Australian news programme, James Randi coached artist José Alvarez to pretend he was channelling a two-thousand-year-old spirit named 'Carlos'. Even after the hoax was revealed, and Carlos was shown to be a fictional character created by Randi and Alvarez, many people continued to believe that 'Carlos' was real. Randi commented: 'No amount of evidence, no matter how good it is or how much there is of it, is ever going to convince the true believer to the contrary.'

Underlying Factors

I am interested in all 'true believer' tales, but especially those of the apocalyptic variety. One of the few consistent features of human civilisation is the presence of people forecasting its imminent termination with great certainty. You can look at any period in history, in any part of the world, and you'll find some cult or fanatical sect that is pretty sure the world is going to end soon, always in a fairly dramatic fashion, and we should all be getting ready. (I have never been entirely sure of the most appropriate way to 'get ready' for my own extinction and that of everyone and everything I have ever known. I sincerely doubt I could ever feel very 'ready' for such a thing. It's not as if there's anything to pack, or that I ought to let the neighbours know that I'll be away for a while.)

In an article published in *Skeptical Inquirer*, psychologist Matthew J Sharps and his colleagues studied the psychology of these apocalyptic faithful. Specifically, they studied their reactions after the world disappoints and befuddles them by failing to come to an end on cue. Using the 2012 Mayan apocalypse prophecy as example, and citing several other similar cases, Sharps identified four psychological factors that compel people to persist with a given belief despite the evidence that it is erroneous.

- **Subclinical dissociative tendencies**. Individuals with subclinical dissociative tendencies are not regarded as suffering from mental illness as such. However, they have a greater than normal tendency to experience disconnection with their immediate physical reality and to be very credulous when considering or assessing what most of us would regard as highly improbable claims. This kind of subclinical dissociation is associated with belief in the paranormal.

- **Cognitive dissonance**. When you invest a great deal in a particular belief, you attach more value to it and therefore become very protective of it. When you face facts or evidence that seem to contradict the belief, you resist this perceived 'attack' on your belief system by any means you can (such as refusing to look at the evidence or resorting to evasive and highly flawed 'reasoning').

- **Gestalt processing**. People with gestalt processing tend to accept an idea as a whole in a rather uncritical way, rather than applying any detailed analysis. (The opposite is feature-intensive thinking.) Sharps suggested a possible relationship between dissociative tendencies and gestalt processing. Those who are inclined to believe various paranormal claims are also more likely to credulously embrace rumours that most people know very little about.

- **Availability heuristic.** People are more likely to believe a particular idea when it's easy to think of relevant supporting examples, for example from recent news bulletins and stories shared online (even if those examples are factually incorrect or misleading). Many people believed in apocalyptic Mayan prophecies because countless news channels and topical magazines ran stories about them. People tend to let their judgement be swayed by the latest news stories and whatever is trending online.

Sleight Of Mind

In this chapter, I've mentioned the parallels between visual illusions that fool the eye and cognitive illusions that fool the mind. The worlds of magic and mentalism present a similar comparison. My many friends and colleagues in the world of magic and stage illusions use misdirection to control where the audience is *looking* at any given moment. There are many different tools of misdirection, such as hand movements, tone of voice and body language.

In my own work as a mentalist I work with thoughts and imagination, and therefore have to go about things in a different way. Instead of trying to misdirect your eyes, my job is to misdirect your thoughts. This is sleight of mind, as opposed to sleight of hand. Cognitive distraction and cognitive illusions are all part of the games I play during every show with every audience.

I never say much about how I do the things I do. If I explained everything, I'd take away a lot of the fun. However, I'll mention just one principle that I often use, and which I used on you in the previous chapter. You may remember that in the previous chapter I asked you to guess the answer to 14 x 37. If you turn back to page 55, you'll see that I said, 'and you're absolutely right (it's actually 519)'. This is untrue: the correct answer is 518.

Some of you may have spotted this at the time, and quietly scoffed at me for my poor arithmetic. However, I can guarantee that most people reading this book will *not* have noticed the deliberate mistake, even though it's plainly impossible for a number with 4 at the end, and a number with 7 at the end, to produce a total ending in 9. Why can I be sure that most readers didn't notice it? Because I buried it inside a paragraph, inside parentheses, and made it seem very unimportant. I followed it with the words, 'What's *fun* and *fascinating* about this...', to get you interested in what was coming next and get you to forget all about the boring arithmetic.

Hidden in Plain Sight

This is a very important element of what I do in my work as a mentalist: I look for ways to hide things in plain sight. I can't actually make a printed number on a page disappear, like the 519 printed on that page in the previous chapter. What I can do is make it disappear *from your mind*, which is the next best thing and achieves the same result. However, I shall say no more about the inner workings of my art.

By the way, if the 519 trick didn't work on you, and you *did* spot my deliberate mistake, I have some good news and some bad news.

The good news is that you are probably a stronger System 2 thinker than most people around you. You have good analytical skills, and are better equipped than most to check facts, think things through and evaluate whether a statement is correct or not. If you want the bad news, look at the text box at the bottom of page 78.

A Change of Perspective

At the very start of this book, I invited you to look at a photo. Most of you will have thought it was a picture of me holding a piece of paper bearing the word 'NITE'.

This is *not* what was in the photo. Honestly.

Now that we have looked at heuristics, System 1 thinking and cognitive illusions, I can reveal the truth: there was *nothing* written on the piece of paper at all. The photos on the opposite page show the true situation.

The letters NITE were *cut out* of the paper. The wall behind me was a plain uniform colour, apart from one dark blue rectangle that was visible *through* the cutout letters.

Your mind decided the word NITE was written on the paper for several very good and fairly obvious reasons. Let's jog through them.

(1) Words are usually *printed* on paper as opposed to being *cut out* from it. In your entire life, you have had untold millions of experiences of the former (words printed on paper) and probably only a handful of the latter (words formed by cutting away).

(2) You have also seen untold millions of walls in your life, and walls usually have some sort of consistent colour or pattern. In the NITE photo, it was reasonable for you to assume that the entire wall behind me was a uniform pale colour.

(3) As will be obvious, this NITE illusion only works from one specific point of view, when the cut-out letters in the paper happen to line up with the blue rectangle behind me. Once again, this is not your normal experience of life. In normal life, ascertaining what is written on a piece of paper or a sign does not depend on your perspective or alignment.

So there were at least three factors, based on your experience of life, that led you to a conclusion that was perfectly reasonable... but unfortunately incorrect.

What does this have to do with persuasion? Everything. Next time you want to persuade someone that something is true, start with this NITE illusion. I wanted you to think I was holding up a piece of paper with the word NITE on it. I asked myself if I could think of three things in your own experience of life, and your own experience of perceiving the world around you, that would assist with this gentle deception.

I thought of the three factors listed above (words are normally printed / walls are normally uniform / perspective and alignment are usually irrelevant). I then used these three pieces of data, concerning *your* mind and how *you* habitually perceive the world, to create the deceptive image.

The important point is that I found the persuasive tools I needed in *your* head, not in mine. *You* provided everything I needed to lead you to see and think what I *wanted* you to see and think.

When you want to persuade someone about anything, try going through the same exercise. Think about the person you want to persuade. What can you find in *their* mind, in *their* thoughts and feelings, in *their* experience of forming perceptions about the world, that you can use in *your* favour?

It doesn't really matter to anyone whether they think I'm holding up a piece of paper with NITE on it. This is a trivial illusion, but I have used it to illustrate a *process* of persuasive and manipulative thinking that is not trivial at all.

When you fully appreciate and understand the NITE illusion, and the thinking behind it, you will also understand every successful persuasive process you have ever seen, or been affected by, in your entire life. This includes every successful advertising campaign, business negotiation, political victory, seduction or bargaining process.

One last word. About 10-15% of you, when you looked at the photo, will also have concluded that the word was 'printed' in black ink. It isn't. The rectangular patch on the wall behind me in the photo was a dark blue, but it was definitely not black. However, this dark blue, coupled with the word 'NITE', will have been enough for *some* of you to have perceived it as black. This is a relatively minor effect, which as I say will only have affected a small percentage of you, but it's an interesting additional factor in the illusion.

And that's the story of the NITE picture.

I have just told you that your ability to spot my 519 trick means you have good analytical skills, are better equipped than most to check facts... and so on. I expect you felt strongly inclined to believe this.

Well, sorry, but that was also untrue.

It is quite impossible, on the basis of one single little trick in a book like this, to say anything at all about your analytical abilities or anything else. For all I know, it could just have been a fluke. For all I know, you only ever spot one erroneous 'fact' in a thousand, and have all the analytical sophistication of a scalded cat. But it felt convincing at the time, didn't it, not to say pleasantly flattering? Welcome to the persuasion game!

Gilan's Persuasion Tips

Here are three simple tips for you based on this chapter:

- Appreciate the power of cognitive illusions, and see if you can put them to good use in your persuasive strategies, for example by using scarcity marketing, or by shaping your message to appeal to what people *want* to be true.

- Be aware of the persistence of myth (even in the face of facts). It may take a lot of effort to establish a myth, or a sales message, but it's worth it if the myth endures — which it usually will.

- Study the thinking behind the NITE example and use it to help you shape and develop your own persuasive plans. Which ideas already present in the other person's mind can you use?

Summary

The preceding chapter referred to times when System 2 thinking fails to override faulty System 1 thinking, and two common causes: cognitive distractions and cognitive illusions.

This short chapter explored the second of these two causes: cognitive illusions. We saw how they are, in many ways, more persistent than visual illusions, and ventured into the strange world of 'true believers' to see why this might be so.

Just as there is a comparison between visual and cognitive illusions, I also touched briefly on the comparison between stage magic which relies on sleight of hand, and mentalism which relies of sleight of mind. I briefly mentioned a favourite principle of mine: hiding things in plain sight. The basic idea is that I may not be able to make something invisible to your eyes, but I can make it invisible to your mind.

In the next chapter, I want to look at one of the greatest and most fundamental of all mental illusions. It all starts with one question. How could a psychic, meeting a complete stranger for the first time, correctly identify that person's new job and even name her new boss? How indeed...

7: The Mirage of Meaning

"I would rather try to persuade a man to go along, because once I have persuaded him, he will stick. If I scare him, he will stay just as long as he is scared, and then he is gone."

— *Dwight D Eisenhower*

Meaning in Mist

One of the reasons I study cold reading so much, and with such abiding interest, is that it provides so many insights into the mechanisms of persuasion.

Consider this example. A client has been to see a psychic and comes back very favourably impressed. She says, 'The psychic was amazing! She somehow knew that I have just changed jobs, and that my new boss is called Sarah! Isn't that incredible?'

If the psychic had, indeed, been able to glean these facts just by staring at tarot cards or the palm of someone's hand then, yes, I'd be the first to sing her praises. However, this is not necessarily what happened during this delightful encounter. There is at least one possible alternative explanation. It is perhaps equally impressive in its own way, just slightly bereft of psychic powers. Had we been able to observe what actually happened at the reading, we might have witnessed something like the following.

Psychic: 'Looking at the cards, I can see this is a time of change and transition for you, perhaps to do with a change of scene, or travel, or the pursuit of new knowledge. Could this apply to you, or is it to someone you know?'

Client: 'I'm not sure. I can't think of anything.'

Psychic: 'That's okay, it's just an impression that might mean something significant or it might not. I'm just picking up on a sense of a change of perspective, like passing from one chapter in your life to another. Maybe this isn't you, it's someone you know.'

Client: 'Well, I've just started a new job, could that be it?'

Psychic: 'Yes, that's probably what it is. I mean, a new job certainly involves change, doesn't it?'

Client: 'Oh, I see. Yes, I suppose so.'

The point is that the psychic didn't know about the new job, the *client* did. The client took the psychic's words about change and new scenes, which could be applied to hundreds of different life events, and found something they could relate to: a new job.

What about the impressive divination of the name 'Sarah'? This could have come about via a similar process. It is possible that during the reading the psychic mentioned dozens of common male and female names. Some of them meant nothing to the client (and were forgotten), but there were one or two that, purely by chance, she could connect to someone in her life — such as her new boss.

Facts in Fantasy

I admit that the example I have just given is hypothetical. However, I have seen precisely this kind of exchange in many psychic readings, and have used these strategies in readings I have given myself (purely for research purposes). I respectfully suggest it is typical of the kind of thing that goes on during the vast majority of psychic readings. What's interesting is that this kind of exchange can take place *without* anyone knowingly trying to deceive anyone else. It is perfectly possible for both parties to be utterly sincere — one trying to deliver psychic insights for her client's benefit, the other trying her best to interpret the sometimes fairly vague glimmers of understanding in a helpful way.

What the psychic is doing, in essence, is providing plenty of noisy, ambiguous data, and allowing the client to sift through it and find any meaning or significance she can. If you have tried to spot castles in clouds, you know the sort of things I mean.

Although I don't give readings professionally, I do occasionally dabble with cold reading whenever I'm presented with a good opportunity to do so. For me, it's a bit of practice to make sure I don't get too rusty.

I was at a speaker showcase addressing about seven-hundred event organisers and corporate clients. During lunch, I caught up with an old friend of mine, whom I hadn't seen in ages. After a little chat, I decided to have a bit of fun with cold reading. I said, 'So, how's work going?' 'Good,' she replied. 'Why do I sense there's been a change or a transition of some sort?' My friend looked startled and said, 'You've been speaking to Louise (a mutual friend) haven't you?' This was not the case, and I had no idea what my friend had found so startling, but I just carried on with my 'reading'. 'You're feeling cautiously optimistic,' I said. 'Why would that be?'

Our conversation lasted about twenty minutes. At the end of it, my old friend went away convinced that I knew every little detail of her plans and that our mutual friend must have provided me with lots of personal information. In point of fact, I had scarcely any idea how anything I had said related to anything going on in my friend's life. All I could guess was that she was thinking of starting up her own new venture, but she was a little hesitant because she had tried and failed once before. But that was okay because I didn't have to find the links between my words and her life — that was *her* job, and she seemed to be very good at it given how impressed she was by my 'insight'.

I offered a lot of dots, and allowed my friend to join any of them up into any pattern she wanted (and ignore the rest). It's remarkable that this simple process, the underlying mechanism of the psychic industry, has been happily uniting psychics and clients since the dawn of human civilisation.

Castles in Clouds

Your brain is superb at detecting patterns and learning to recognise them. This is an essential survival skill, so it's not surprising that the brain has evolved to be rather good at it. Unfortunately, the brain is so determined to find patterns that it can even find them when they aren't there. This is why people think they see images in inkblots, clouds and toasted waffles. Stare at random shades and textures for long enough, and you're sure to discover faces, figures and objects.

When I was a child, my friends and I played a game that involved trying to see shapes and pictures in clouds. One of us would mention a particular theme or subject, and we would all try to find a shape in the clouds that seemed to match it. I don't think I can remember a single time when this did *not* work. The clouds were very obliging, and always seemed ready to rearrange themselves into whatever shapes we were looking for at the time. I am sure you have probably played similar games at some point in your life.

Even the supposedly brightest among us can perceive meaning where there is none. This was demonstrated in a wonderful experiment conducted by Donald Naftulin and colleagues from the University of Southern California. The day before an academic conference, they wrote a nonsensical paper on 'Mathematical Game Theory as Applied to Physician Education'. This paper was complete gibberish from start to finish. They then hired an actor to present this paper to the conference, introducing him as 'Dr Myron L Fox'.

After 'Dr Fox' presented his meaningless paper, there was a thirty-minute question-and-answer session during which he fielded questions from the audience of psychiatrists, psychologists and social workers. According to Naftulin's account, his answers consisted of, 'double talk, non sequiturs and contradictory statements.' Subsequently, the audience were asked to rate and review the talk and the feedback was *excellent*. The serious, thoughtful conference delegates found not just meaning in the meaningless fake talk by the fake expert, but also insight and expertise.

We ought not to be too surprised that the brain has evolved in such a way as to make false positive errors (see shapes that aren't there) rather than false negative errors (not see shapes that *are* there). From a survival point of view, it is more important to see a few patterns that are not actually there than to miss the one that is. Is that a tiger in the bush, or just a breeze?

From Delusion to Persuasion

This intriguing 'castles in clouds' phenomenon has many obvious lessons for anyone interested in persuasion games.

Persuasion is often assumed to be like this: I make a statement and try to get you to believe that I'm right. But it can just as often be like this: I offer a lot of noisy data, and let you persuade yourself that I'm right.

If I am discussing a complex business deal with you, I could try to argue my case very rationally and logically, point by point, trying to more or less force you to agree that I'm right and we should do the deal my way. I doubt this strategy would be very effective. People only love good reasoning when it leads to where they want to get to.

Alternatively, I could start by figuring out what you would like to believe. For example, you might like to believe that you're getting the upper hand, or that you're getting a much better price than anyone else, or that doing this deal will make you shine in the eyes of your boss or… whatever the case may be. My job, then, is to give you enough bits and pieces of data to allow you to join the dots your way, and reach the conclusion you want to come to. I could talk about past projects, costings, materials, legal issues, scheduling, logistics, personnel… just about anything that has any bearing on the project. All that matters is that I give you enough clay to build whatever pot you want to create. This may not be a very logical approach, but it is a very persuasive one. The success of every psychic since the dawn of recorded time is not a mysterious fluke. It's persuasion science in action, and we can learn good lessons accordingly.

Inhibited Ambiguity

This fascinating 'false positive' bias has given rise to the rather wonderful term 'inhibited ambiguity'. Take a look at this:

On the left side of the picture, you see the letters ABC. On the right side, you see the numbers 12, 13, 14. The central figure in both cases is identical — it is an ambiguous couple of lines that can be seen as either a letter or a number.

If you see these lines in isolation, you can probably see them as what they are: ambiguous. However, when you see them in a specific context (whether it's letters or numbers) your ability to perceive the ambiguity is inhibited. It becomes very difficult for you to see it as anything except a letter B or the number 13.

Here's another example. Consider the sentence: 'Judy was a bit disappointed when she looked at the scales'. What do you imagine Judy is doing? If you try to envisage the scene, what do you see? Most people imagine a woman who is in the process of weighing herself and isn't too pleased with her current weight. This picture can come to mind very easily, because every single day there are countless references to weight loss tips and tricks all over the media, as well as controversies about 'size zero' models and how women are depicted in advertising.

However, there are other ways to interpret the sentence that are just as plausible, but less likely to spring to mind.

What would happen in your mind if I had first of all mentioned that Judy was cleaning a fish to prepare it for cooking? Now your mind suddenly adopts a completely different scenario. Judy is taking a close look at the fish and she's a bit disappointed with its quality or freshness. It's a perfectly legitimate way to interpret the sentence, but the 'standing on the scales and checking her weight' scenario came to mind far more easily.

This gets very interesting when you see the same phenomenon arising in other contexts. For example, when people with strong beliefs are presented with *ambiguous* information relevant to their views, they struggle to see the ambiguity. They see what they want to see, or (more precisely) whatever provides the strongest support for their pre-existing belief.

You have probably seen this phenomenon in many informal, social settings. Rugby is an extremely popular sport in South Africa, inspiring passionate team loyalty. I was once watching a game between the Sharks and the Lions with two friends with loyalties to the opposing teams. The referee called a foul. One friend exclaimed, 'That was *never* a foul! That tackle was *perfectly* fair and above board!' My other friend said, 'It was *clearly* a foul — just look how low it was!' They had both just seen the exact same event, but what they perceived was skewed by their respective team loyalty. I doubt there's a major sporting event in history that has not been accompanied by many similar disputes of interpretation. This is, so I'm told, part of the fun.

Inhibited ambiguity isn't such a problem when it only leads to friends shouting about the fairness or otherwise of a referee's call. But it can be a very significant problem indeed in other contexts — religion, politics and eyewitness testimony to name but three. There are many times in the affairs of our species when it would be tremendously useful if people could say, 'I know that looks one way to me, but I expect it's actually ambiguous and I'm just being biased by own beliefs.' Alas, this seldom happens.

Consistency Is King

Inhibited ambiguity leads to all manner of misunderstandings and false conclusions. But there's another factor that assists the formation of delusional conclusions (to coin a phrase). It turns out that System 1 thinking is insensitive to both the quality and the quantity of the information it processes. It places more emphasis on the *consistency* of information rather than its completeness.

In other words, when you are in System 1 mode, you are interested in whether the new data is consistent with, or can be *made* to be consistent with, what you already know. If one interpretation leads to, 'This doesn't fit, we have a problem, we need a rethink', and the other leads to, 'This confirms what we already know', the second interpretation will win every time. Remember that since we're talking about System 1 thinking, this can all happen in a flash without you really having much awareness of it at all. You simply feel you have seen the 'correct' interpretation, when in fact your System 1 thinking has selected whichever interpretation means you don't have to rethink anything.

These tendencies we have to perceive meaning in ambiguity and prize consistency above all else can lead us to accept a given statement as true, rather than seeing it as *either* false *or* too vague to mean anything and lacking in significance.

The bad news doesn't end there. Once your brain has perceived the meaning it wants to perceive, and favoured consistency above all else, it will adhere to the resulting interpretation with fierce stubbornness. This grants you the luxury of not having to think hard about the issue anymore. This has an important bearing on the subject of compliance, which we'll look at in Chapter 11.

Narrative Fallacy

So far, we have looked at a few of the ways in which you can arrive at a false perception of meaning, or a biased conclusion. However, this does not just affect what you think here and now — it will affect how you recall the past, and what expectation you have of the future.

When you recall past events, especially ones that involve some sort of evaluation or interpretation, you will be unlikely to recall what actually happened and more likely to recall whichever interpretation suited you at the time. Consider the story I mentioned of my two friends arguing over a disputed call during a rugby game. The first friend will not remember an ambiguous bit of action from the game, but will actually remember a fair tackle followed by a hopelessly bad call by the referee. This didn't happen, but it *is* now his memory of the event.

This is known as the narrative fallacy. The story or narrative that you construct, and associate with a past event, becomes the reality of that event *for you*, regardless of whether it's the reality for anyone else.

This is why I never argue with anyone about what they say happened during a psychic reading. I may have very good reasons to suspect that their account does not match what actually took place. However, I know their account perfectly matches *the only memory they have* of the reading. For that person, their own recollection of the event *is* the reality of what happened. They have no access to any other version.

There is an obvious lesson here for all students of persuasion games. If I can persuade you of a particular point of view *once*, the chances are I've persuaded you for ever. This is why it can be worth quite an investment of time and effort to achieve that first moment of successful persuasion. Putting it another way, this is why it's worth spending vast fortunes of money advertising fizzy drinks, sports shoes and brands of clothing to young, impressionable minds. A lifetime of unthinking consumer loyalty provides a good return on investment.

Hindsight Bias

An interesting corollary to the narrative fallacy is hindsight bias, which can be instantly recognised by the phrase, 'I knew it all along'. Since you tend not to recall past events as they *actually* happened, but adhere to your *constructed narrative* of what happened, it is easy to persuade yourself that you knew more than you did, or were surprised less than you really were.

It's easy to see the allure of this kind of self-delusion. If you think of yourself as an expert on the economy, it suits your purpose to be able to look back over a period of economic activity, particularly one that contained a few surprises, and to nod sagely to yourself as you tell everyone you knew what would happen all along.

Psychologists have studied this effect many times. In one experiment, a researcher got a group of students to discuss a controversial subject on which they had not completely made up their mind, such as atomic weapons. First, he carefully measured everyone's initial opinion on the matter. He then showed everyone a very persuasive video arguing the case for (or against) the subject under discussion, after which he assessed everyone's opinion once more. Many of the students were now more sympathetic to the opinion presented in the video. The researcher asked those who had most significantly changed their mind to recall how they had felt about the issue originally, before the experiment began. Many found this surprisingly difficult to do. When asked to reconstruct their former beliefs, people retrieved their *current* beliefs instead — a simple case of substitution. Some found it difficult to believe they had ever felt differently.

Persuasion Lessons

These insights into how people form their views and opinions can help you to become a better persuader, and also save you a lot of time.

In many situations, you may not need to argue your case very convincingly, point by point. It may be enough to offer ambiguous data in which the other person can see whatever they want to see.

A very good example of this occurs in adverts for investment companies. The deal with an investment company is this: you give them a lot of your money, and after a period of time you might get more back than you put in, or you might get less. What's more, the companies have to state that this is the case in their advertising (at least they do in most of the well-regulated financial markets). Up or down, win or lose, they can't guarantee what will happen and neither can you.

However, what they can do is offer you ambiguous data, such as an image of the large, impressive skyscraper they call head office. There are a few ways to see this image:

- This company is big and impressive. They must be very good at what they do. I can trust them with my money.

- Look at how much money these people have managed to gouge out of their clients: enough to build this nice, comfy office building regardless of whether their clients made money or lost everything.

- Why is this company trying to distract me with meaningless pictures of a big office block, when all that matters is whether I will make money by investing with them, and what evidence they can provide to support this contention?

The majority of potential investors tend to see the first option, because of the obvious inherent bias: you want to have a big, powerful company on *your* side, working *for* you, to deliver significant profits while you don't even lift a finger?

In brief, the art of persuasion often has nothing to do with trying to present a coherent, compelling argument. In many cases, you just have to provide the clouds, and give people room to see what they want to see.

Gilan's Persuasion Tips

Here are three simple tips for you based on this chapter:

- Understand that people often see meaning where none exists. Maybe you don't have to offer a convincing argument — just sufficient clouds for people to convince themselves.

- Consistency is king. If you want me to believe X, show me that X is consistent with what I already know / think / feel / believe / want to be true.

- Thanks to the narrative fallacy, it's largely true that you only have to convince someone *once* to convince them *for ever*. So it may be worth making a big effort to achieve that initial persuasive success.

Summary

In this chapter, we looked at the 'castles in clouds' phenomenon of people seeing meaning that isn't there.

We looked at the rather intriguing notion of 'inhibited ambiguity', i.e. not being able to see that something is neutral and open to interpretation (such as the letter B or the number 13), and only being able to see the interpretation we want.

We saw how this effect can lead to false memories, and the so-called narrative fallacy of confusing your constructed memory of an event with the reality of what happened. This, in turn, can lead to hindsight bias, the rather self-congratulatory phenomenon of thinking you had much more insight than you really did.

Of course, you really don't need to worry about finding meaning or interpreting data if you can rely on something far better: your intuition. After all, intuition is fairly magical stuff that never lets you down... right?

As it happens, this is the subject of the next chapter. It all starts with a very simple question with a very difficult answer...

Gilan Smile.

This photo is referred to on page 2 of this book.

Choose 1 From 5.

This graphic is referred to on page 23 of this book.

Look at the chart and say the COLOUR not the word

BLACK WHITE GREY

WHITE **GREY WHITE**

BLACK WHITE **GREY**

WHITE GREY BLACK

Stroop Test

This graphic is referred to on page 62 of this book.

8: Intuition

"Persuasion can go through obstacles that force cannot."

— Yusef A Leing

The Joy of Intuition

It's playtime! Have a look at this picture of four cards.

Suppose I make this claim about the four cards: every card that has an even number on one side has a picture of a bear on the other side.

Which card or cards would you need to turn over to see if my claim is true? It's worth having a good think about this before you read the rest of this chapter. I'll give you the correct answer a little later on.

Guess and Yes

We can loosely define your intuition as your faculty for making educated guesses based on past experience and emotions. In a previous chapter, we looked at 'fast' System 1 thinking. Your intuition can be seen as your System 1 thinking going on in the background, constantly collecting new data and trying to distil new knowledge from it.

When you 'listen to your intuition', it feels less like an intellectual, analytical process and more of a 'feeling' that fills your mind and your body. This is why people often use expressions such as, 'I can feel it in my gut', or 'I knew in my bones that I couldn't trust him'.

Your intuition guides your beliefs, actions and responses more or less all the time. There's no doubt that your intuition *can* be very useful in many circumstances. Sometimes you have to make a judgement or a decision before you have all the relevant facts, and your intuition is more or less all you have to go on.

This being the case, it would be marvellous if your intuition were an infallible guide to reality. Unfortunately, this is not the case. It *can* lead you astray.

Confirmation Bias

One very well known flaw of intuition is a confirmation bias: the tendency to only seek confirmation of an existing belief, rather than actually examining whether it's true.

To see how this works, imagine I'm talking with my imaginary friend Mike. We happen to mention America, and Mike mentions that he has a hunch that every American state begins with the letter N.

Mike finds a map of America.

He points to Nebraska and thinks to himself, 'My theory is off to a pretty good start.'

Then he points to North Carolina and Nevada, and thinks, 'There must be something to this.'

Next, he points to New Hampshire and North Dakota. He says, 'I guess I've pretty much proved my case… I doubt there's much point checking anything else'.

Just to be thorough, and so that nobody can accuse him of rushing to lazy conclusions, he points to two more states: New Mexico and New York. He congratulates himself on the accuracy of his original hunch.

I say to Mike, 'Okay, but are you *really* sure? Can you really be so certain?'

Just to indulge me, Mike gives out a wistful sigh and turns to the map once more. He looks over it, then points to New Jersey. 'See?', he says, 'my theory checks out. I told you I'm never wrong about these things.'

I'm sure this little hypothetical scene strikes you as utterly absurd, since it's clear that a great many American states begin with letters other than N. Unfortunately, even though it *is* absurd, confirmation bias is *very* common. Even psychologists and psychiatrists, who know about confirmation bias, can still be guilty of it.

In 1967 psychologist husband and wife team, Loren and Jean Chapman, devised an interesting experiment. Their area of interest was the Draw a Picture psychiatric assessment test. They took a series of patient drawings, and some lists of symptoms, and paired them up *randomly*. There was no correspondence between the symptoms and the drawing. They showed these to experienced psychiatric professionals, claiming that they were genuine case studies. The psychiatrists proceeded to explain how the correct interpretation of the drawings did, indeed, correlate with the symptoms of the patient in almost every case. In other words, when they knew what the answer was supposed to be (the supplied set of symptoms), they could find a way to interpret the drawing accordingly. This was a very clear case of confirmation bias, suggesting that this particular diagnostic tool was next to worthless.

Sixth Sense and Supercops

There are many different kinds of intuition, but there are two in particular that I'm interested in because they crop up time and again in my work. They are what I call 'sixth sense' intuition, which we'll look at now, and 'speed reasoning' intuition, which we'll get to in a few pages.

So what's 'sixth sense' intuition all about?

A team of firefighters is tackling a blazing building. They enter a room, and perform a quick visual check for their own safety. All seems well — there are no signs of any structural damage, and no reason to think they are in any great danger. Nonetheless, the team leader suddenly issues a firm order for everyone to evacuate the room and get clear. Moments later, the roof collapses.

Here's another story in similar vein.

The police have impounded a car which they suspect was used in a crime. Two detectives have been checking it over, examining it for any forensic clues that might help them crack the case. After a thorough check, they find nothing. They report to their senior officer, who tells them to go back and check the car again, as he's sure they'll find something. They do so, and find nothing. He tells them he's still sure about it, and makes them go back to check the car a third time. They find the crucial speck of evidence they need to make their case.

There are countless well-documented examples of this kind of 'sixth sense' intuition, in just about every professional field. The key factor in these examples is that of *recognition*. Specifically, recognition of the patterns that arise in their work. The more experience you have of these patterns, the more of a 'sixth sense' you will seem to have to everyone around you. You will be able to spot patterns that others cannot because they haven't accumulated your depth of experience. You will also be able to anticipate events more accurately, and more completely, than they can.

The Chess Instinct

In my research for this book, I became fascinated by the work of American psychologist and polymath Herbert Simon, winner of the 1978 Nobel Memorial Prize in Economics. Simon studied many different fields, but the unifying theme to most of his work was his passionate desire to understand decision-making and the processes by which both good and bad decisions get made. In his work on problem-solving behaviour, Simon made an extensive study of chess players. He showed that chess grandmasters, after thousands of hours of practice and professional tournaments, come to see the pieces on the board differently from the rest of us. He said:

> *"The situation has provided a cue; this cue has given the expert access to information stored in memory, and the information provides the answer. Intuition is nothing more and nothing less than recognition."*

Although I was never a chess grandmaster, I can relate to what Simon is describing. When I first started playing chess, I had to think long and hard before I could figure out the best move. As my knowledge and skill developed, and as I started to build up my experience, I began to feel as if I just intuitively knew what the best move was, almost without having to think about it at all.

Playbook Mastery

Here's another example from a very different arena. John Maxwell, in his book, *21 Irrefutable Laws of Leadership*, has a section on The Law of Intuition. He mentions the example of quarterbacks in American Football who memorise every single play by heart so that during the game their intuition would take over at intense moments when vital decisions had to be made instantly. They made it their business to develop their intuition. A coach said:

> *"I can't rely on the playbook. There isn't time. You see, by the time the ball carrier's knee touches the ground, I have to know what play to call next based on the situation. There's no time to fumble around deciding what to do."*

No matter what your field of expertise, as you build up your experience you start to develop your gift of 'sixth sense' intuition. What's interesting about this is the interplay between what we described as System 1 thinking (fast) and System 2 thinking (slow). Your System 1 thinking can derive legitimate patterns and lessons from your experience *before your System 2 has learned to name or recognise them.* In other words, you acquire some valid and helpful information before the slow, rational, analytical System 2 thinking has had a chance to assimilate it in its own terms. This is what gives rise to the slightly strange feeling of being able to 'know' something even if you can't rationally account for it.

This also tallies with my personal experience learning judo. My sensei (teacher) said that Judo is like chess: you have to anticipate what your move is going to be, then how your opponent will respond, then how you're going to counter, and so on. However, you have to know all this instinctively. The only way to achieve this 'instinct' is to have lots and lots of fights in the judo ring. Intuition may be a type of shortcut, but there are no shortcuts to acquiring it. These things take time!

Reading Matters

Even if we don't all turn out to be 'supercops' or excel in our chosen profession, we have all been through the process of slowly acquiring experience that leads to a sense of knowing things on the intuitive level.

For example, when you first started learning to read as a child, it took plenty of effort just to work out each individual letter and then put them together to form a word. In later life, you read your native language so effortlessly that you have no sense at all of breaking each word down into letters and sounds. it all seems to happen effortlessly, as if you merely glance at the words and the author's meaning is clear in your mind — in other words, it seems to happen intuitively.

However, as soon as you start trying to learn a new language as an adult, you are instantly reminded of the very complex process you have to go through to slowly, patiently process written information and extract some meaning from it.

As with words and reading, so it is with *people* and *situations*. When you are young, you haven't had time to develop many social skills so it can sometimes be hard to respond appropriately to people, especially when you meet them for the first time, or to unfamiliar situations. As you grow into adulthood, and build your experience of life, you become more adept at getting along with people and handling new or unfamiliar situations a little way out of your comfort zone.

Perils of Confidence

'Supercop' stories and the like are all very well, but we have to remember that 'sixth sense' intuition does not always work very successfully. It can lead some people to be overconfident in their ability or judgement, and to place far more faith in their 'hunches' than they ought to.

For example, a keen, ambitious young stockbroker might get a new job and make three or four judgement calls that turn out to be correct. He begins to feel that he has an amazing, profound understanding of the markets, and can do no wrong. The reality is far more dull — he just happened to get lucky three or four times in a row. Supremely confident of his innate (but sadly non-existent) talent, he undertakes a particularly large gamble on the markets... and loses everything.

Overconfidence is not just a problem for those who suffer from it, but for everyone else they do business with. We tend to warm towards very confident people. One definition of 'charisma' is 'the aura generated by total confidence, unhampered by self-doubt'. Most of us harbour some level of self-doubt, even if only over minor things that don't really matter. To meet someone who enjoys, or who seems to enjoy, total self-confidence without any form of self-doubt feels refreshing and a little invigorating. We can't help thinking it would be nice to be like them, to never be held back by doubt or insecurity of any kind. Hence that feeling of 'charisma', of 'I want to be like that person'.

However, if we warm to someone based on their strong self-confidence, and this confidence turns out to be exaggerated and built on foundations of sand, it can lead to problems. Every year, many people hand over money they can't afford to lose to 'investment experts', largely based on the so-called expert's aura of confidence, and end up losing everything. Note that this can happen *even when the 'expert' is sincere*, and doesn't intend to swindle anyone or let them down. Sincerity is no guarantee of excellence, and nor are good intentions.

Sorting Good from Bad

Given that self-confidence can sometimes be misplaced, how can we protect ourselves from the consequences? How can we distinguish the right people to trust (whose confidence is legitimately rooted in experience) from the rest (whose confidence is delusional)?

I won't say I have all the answers, but I can offer some advice. Ask yourself two questions:

- Does this person operate in an environment that is sufficiently predictable for 'expertise' to be a meaningful term?

- Has this person learned *what* he can predict, within that environment, based on substantial experience?

With regard to the first question, consider someone who says he has a way to predict each spin of a roulette wheel. It doesn't matter how confident he may appear — he is claiming to predict that which is by its nature not predictable (which is why you can still find roulette wheels in casinos). He is suggesting to be an expert about something it is not possible to be an expert about. You may safely walk away from both him and his supposed expertise.

With regard to the second question, consider someone yet to achieve his twenty-first birthday who would like to manage your investment portfolio for you. Again, it doesn't matter how radiantly confident he appears to be, or how much 'evidence' he offers of his talent for smart investment. He simply cannot have gained sufficient experience to know what he claims to know. Just walk away, and don't look back.

It is only when *both* these conditions are fulfilled that a person's intuition is likely to be *skilled* and *useful*.

It is worth noting that applying these two 'test' questions is not always easy, and will always involve some subjective assessments. For example, consider the question of what constitutes a predictable environment. I would maintain that chess and poker are both *sufficiently* predictable environments for someone to be able to develop a skilled intuition, but there are some who would disagree about poker. It is clearly an area where you must arrive at your own judgement.

Sixth Sense Psychics

One group of people who definitely *can* lay claim to 'sixth sense' intuition are my friends in the cold reading industry. They pass the two tests with flying colours: they do operate in a sufficiently predictable environment, and the good ones have clearly put in a huge amount of time to learn what is, and is not, predictable within that environment. There can be no question of this, since they prove it every time they give a reading.

It might seem odd to suggest that cold readers work in predictable environment, given that every client is different, every reading is improvised and every reading is unique (and they *will* be unique if the readers concerned are good at what they do). However, within this context of apparently infinite variety, there are sufficient constants to allow the reader to do her job and build up an authentic degree of 'sixth sense' intuition as defined earlier in this section.

For example, someone going for a 'psychic' reading could, hypothetically speaking, want to know about any subject or situation under the sun. In practice, the overwhelming majority of clients want their reading to focus on one or more of just four main themes: career, health, relationships, money (easily remembered as CHaRM). There are also three minor themes that crop up a great deal: travel, education, ambitions (forming the word TEA). If you have learned nothing else from this book, at least you now know that CHaRM and TEA are the basis for 99% of all the psychic readings given in the world today.

Carpet Themes

I should explain in passing that these main themes can all be rolled out as flat as a carpet, and are wide open to interpretation. 'Travel' can be actually getting around by car, train and plane, or going on a journey through life, or a spiritual journey, or a journey into a new relationship (the themes can also be blended and mixed as required). 'Career' can refer to the actual job you do each day, or the one you secretly aspire to do, or something that you do so often that it feels like a job even though it isn't one, or the 'work' of building and sustaining a good relationship (there we go blending again) or your 'spiritual career'… and so on. Psychics rarely let the literal meaning of words constrain their free association of words, ideas and speculation.

As well as building up experience of the main themes that most clients want to hear about, cold readers also develop a good intuitive knowledge of such things as:

- the principal stages in a typical life;

- what clothing and outer appearance may suggest about lifestyle;

- the typical perspectives people tend to have at different times of life.

If you are interested in the first of these — the principal stages in a typical life — you may want to read Gail Sheehy's intriguing book *Passages*, subtitled *The Predictable Crises of Adult Life*. It provides a fascinating distillation of the main stages that most people pass through in their lives.

The Need For Speed

'Speed-reasoning' intuition can be said to derive from two specific kinds of shortcuts: 'substitution' heuristics and 'availability' heuristics. Let's look at each of these in turn.

Substitution Heuristics

Substitution heuristics occur when your brain is faced with a complex or challenging question and substitutes an easier one. They are expressed in terms of the target question (the difficult question or assessment you want to answer) and the substitution question (the one that is easier to answer). For example:

Target question: Is now a good time to invest in Samsung?
Substitution question: Do I like Samsung phones and tablets?

The slightly worrying thing about this process is that it can happen without you being aware of it. You may well not notice that you haven't addressed the target question, and go away believing that you have. Furthermore, you may not be aware that the target question was difficult to answer, since you substituted the easier question so rapidly and instinctively. Clearly, this all presents fertile ground for arguments, disagreements and conflicting accounts of the same events.

This table at the bottom of the page shows some common examples of the substitution heuristic.

Substitution heuristics are yet another factor that help the cold reading industry to survive and thrive. Consider this fairly standard line:

"On the whole, it's fair to say you are more honest than many of the people around you."

If the client were inclined to assess this claim fairly and objectively, it would involve answering this difficult target question: 'How can I measure honesty, and do so using a sufficiently large sample of the population, to see if I tend to be a bit more honest than most?' There is no easy answer.

Here's the substitution question: 'Do I feel I'm more honest than some people I know?'

This is easy to answer: of course you do!

So the client nods and the reading moves forward. Once again, our intrepid cold reader has managed to make a statement to a complete stranger and receive instant confirmation that he is as accurate as an atomic clock.

Original Question	Substituted Question
That man has been nominated for the position of CEO. How high do you think he will climb the corporate ladder?	Does that man look like a corporate winner?
Would you donate money to help preserve wildlife in Africa?	How emotional do I feel about rhinos becoming extinct?
How dangerous is that spider on the wall?	How many times have I heard scary spider stories?
Do you have a good relationship with that person?	How do I feel about that person at this specific moment?

Availability Heuristics

The availability heuristic bases judgements on whichever data most readily comes to mind — not the data that might lead to the best, wisest or more accurate answer.

For example, suppose you conduct a survey where you ask people to nominate the funniest TV sitcom of all time. TV shows that were on in the recent past will tend to get more votes than ones that were broadcast a long time ago. This has nothing to do with whether the more recent shows are or were funnier — they just come to mind more easily.

Similarly, if you canvass people's political opinions and ask them what they think the government should spend more money on, they will either mention an issue that happens to affect them personally, or one that happens to have been in the news a lot lately. Neither personal interest nor recent headlines have much bearing on what ought to be government spending priorities, but they are the easiest things to nominate.

The advertising industry has known about availability heuristics for a long time. The first major oil crisis of modern times, in 1973, produced great swathes of newspaper headlines about the shortage of oil that would probably lead to far higher prices for oil and everything affected by the price of oil — including petrol.

Not long after, adverts for new cars were all careful to make impressive claims about fuel economy. The advertisers knew that 'fuel economy' was going to be a highly 'available' idea in the minds of most consumers, and therefore it made sense to mention this concept in the advertisements. They hadn't bothered to do it in the years before the oil crisis, and when the headlines moved on to newer topics so did the adverts.

In the 1990s, German psychologist Norbert Schwartz devised a fascinating experiment into availability heuristics. He asked a group of students to do two things:

- List six instances in which you behaved assertively.

- Evaluate how assertive you are.

He tried the same experiment with a second group, but this time he asked them to list *twelve* instances, not six. The point is that there are two different factors involved in this task: how many instances you can think of, and how easily they come to mind. If you have just compiled twelve examples of times when you behaved assertively, that's quite a long, impressive list. However, while the first three or four examples probably came to mind fairly quickly and easily, the rest were probably hard to recall and took a lot of effort. For most people, there's less effort involved in just compiling a list of six times when you behaved assertively.

Schwarz wanted to know which of these two factors would prevail: the quantity of evidence or the ease/difficulty of listing it. The result was very clear: people who had just listed twelve instances of assertive behaviour (but had found it difficult to do so) rated themselves as much *less* assertive than those who had only listed six instances (but had not experienced the same difficulty doing so). It seems the feeling of, 'I just found it hard to think of times when I was assertive' leads to the feeling that, 'Maybe I'm just not a very assertive person'. It overrides the feeling of, 'Look at this big, long list I've put together!'.

> *"Self-ratings were dominated by the ease with which examples had come to mind. The experience of fluent retrieval of instances trumped the number retrieved."*

This priming effect plays its part in cold reading. Suppose the psychic says something like this: 'I sense that in the last several months, there have been a few times when you've had to be assertive — I'm sure you can think of a handful of these times — and I sense that you can be quite an assertive person when you need to be.'

'I'm sure you can think of a handful of these times' may seem like a statement, but actually it is designed to have the same effect as, 'List six instances in which you behaved assertively'. By first priming the client to think of several instances of assertive behaviour, the psychic ensures that when he says, 'you are actually quite an assertive person' this will sound like an accurate observation. Another incredible hit for the powers of psychic divination!

Egocentric Bias

We have looked at the 'speed reasoning' type of intuition, and two of its components: the 'substitution' heuristic and the 'availability' heuristic.

The effects of these heuristics is reinforced or amplified by another factor called egocentric bias. This may sound like another slice of academic jargon, but it's really an idea you are already familiar with, and I have two examples for you.

First example: ever noticed how when things go well people take the credit, but when they don't they blame everyone else? That's egocentric bias in action.

You may feel quite sure that other people tend to do this far more than *you* do. This feeling is *also* egocentric bias in action, so that's my second example.

This bias gives rise to all sorts of distorted perceptions: I'm a much more careful driver than other drivers; I waste far less time staring into my phone than my partner; I am far more punctual than other people.

It also gives rise to many humorous 'verbs of irregular conjugation', in which the same thing is seen from three different perspectives:

I drink in moderation to be sociable / you tend to hit the bottle / he's a raging alcoholic.

I made a few slips filling in my expenses sheet / you fiddle the system a bit / he's an outright crook.

Egocentric bias is not just well supported anecdotally — there's some real science involved. For example, researchers once set up interviews with couples who had been married for a long time. They asked both parties to estimate what percentage of the housework they did. The combined total from almost every pair exceeded 100%. Each partner had displayed an egocentric bias by focusing on their own work and downplaying their partner's contribution.

Many other statistics tell the same story. When interviewed, 94% of people think they have an above average sense of humour; 80% of drivers say they are more skilled than the average driver (this is even true of those who are in hospital after a car crash); 75% of business people see themselves as more ethical than the average businessman.

The Downside

In many ways, egocentric bias is good for you. It helps you to feel positive about yourself, to forgive your own faults and failings and to cope with the slings and arrows of outrageous fortune. The downside is that it leaves you wide open to exploitation and manipulation. How so? Well, if I ascribe just about any positive attribute to you, especially when compared with people in general, you are likely to think I'm making sense. I could tell you that you are a little more cooperative, considerate, responsible, friendly, reliable, resourceful, polite or dependable than the average person, and you would probably feel inclined to believe me.

Of course, this wouldn't work on *you* quite as well as it would work on most people. I say this because you're a little bit more shrewd, rational and honest about yourself than most people around you. (See what I did there?)

Cold Ego

Not surprisingly, cold readers use this strategy to their advantage. However, there's a little bit more to it than just saying nice things to the client.

First of all, the flattery needs to be subtle. Rather than saying, 'You're an extremely honest person', the reader will couch it in more moderate terms, like this: 'On the whole, you tend to be a little more honest than many people around you. We all indulge in harmless, little white lies from time to time, even if only to be tactful, but when it comes to important things you have learned that honesty is the best policy.'

Secondly, as noted above, the technique works better if the flattery is stated in comparative terms rather than absolute ones. Rather than offer, 'You are a very considerate and loving partner', he'll say, 'In relationships, you tend to be rather more considerate and loving than many people; it's just in your nature.'

By following these two guidelines, a skilled cold reader can rest assured that every 'flattery' statement he offers will be accepted as 'true' or 'accurate'.

These same techniques work outside the cold reading context. In any situation, whether social or professional, a little bit of flattery goes a long way. Just remember: keep it subtle, and make it comparative rather than absolute.

Mood Food

Before we leave the wonderful world of intuition, I'd like to mention one more factor that plays a part in how intuition operates: your mood. Research suggests that if you are in a good mood, you are more inclined to rely on System 1 thinking, which in turn suggests you are more likely to be guided by your intuition.

In the 1960s Professor Sarnoff Mednick theorised that 'creativity' is the effect of a very high functioning associative memory. To test this theory he devised what is known as the Remote Association Test (RAT) which is still in use today and has even been the basis for some games.

Here's how a RAT works. I give you three words, and you try to think of one word that can be associated with all three of them. Let's try an easy one:

Cream / Skate / Cube

Not too hard, is it? The answer is 'Ice'. (Ice cream, ice skating, ice cube.) Let's try another:

Dust / Cereal / Fish

This is not quite as obvious, but I expect you probably still got the correct answer, which is 'Bowl'. Now try this tough one:

Tooth, Potato, Heart

Don't feel too bad if you didn't get that one — it's very difficult. In an experiment, only 20% of the participants could find the answer in 15 seconds or less. (The correct solution is 'Sweet'.)

It is clearly possible to create a 'fake' RAT, by which I mean a set of three words that do *not* have a solution. This gives rise to an interesting question: can people 'know' intuitively that there *is* a solution to one of these tests, even if they don't actually know what the solution is? Psychologists have looked into this by preparing a series of RATs, some that have a solution and some that do not, and asking participants to guess intuitively whether each one is solvable.

What they found was that the number of correct guesses was far higher than chance would allow. This suggests there is some kind of 'signal' from the associative parts of the brain that detects a connection between what may seem to be random words, even if the precise nature of that connection hasn't been identified.

This was further demonstrated in another experiment where volunteers were simply asked to read groups of words and push the spacebar on their keyboards when they were done. Amazingly, after reading a triad of words that had a solution, the participants had a slight smile, while triads with no solution resulted in no movement or electrical impulses in the facial muscles at all.

Researchers also investigated whether mood has an impact on solving ability. They divided their participants into three groups. One group of volunteers was put in a good mood (for example by asking them to reflect on happy times in their lives and giving them very positive feedback), while another group was put in a bad mood (by doing the opposite). There was also a control group which did not go through any specific mood preparation.

The 'bad mood' participants were unable to guess whether a RAT had a solution with any accuracy — in fact, they scored no better than chance. The 'good mood' volunteers were far more accurate. This suggests that your mood has a direct effect on your System 1 thinking, in that it impedes your 'intuition'. When you are in a good mood, you are inclined to trust your intuition and it works well for you. When you are uncomfortable and unhappy, you lose touch with your intuition.

In the Mood

Cold readers have known about the link between mood and System 1 intuitive thinking for a long time. Before they begin the actual reading, they use several different strategies to manipulate the client's mood so that she is using her System 1 mode of thinking, and hence will be more receptive to the psychic experience.

These strategies include creating a warm, welcoming and somewhat intimate environment, subtly establishing the reader's credentials and 'expertise', adopting a relaxed tone of voice that sets the client at ease, and neutralising any fears the client may have about bad news coming up or having her privacy invaded.

Encouraging the client to use mostly System 1 thinking makes it easier for her to think creatively and find links between the reader's statements and current or past events in her life.

Four Cards Solution

Before we end this chapter, here's the answer to the problem I posed right at the start.

Remember, the claim was: 'Every card that has an even number on one side has a picture of a bear on the other side.'

Which of these cards would you need to turn over to see if my claim is true?

The correct answer is that you would have to turn over two cards.

You would have to turn over the card bearing a number 2. If this doesn't have a bear on the other side, then you know my claim is false.

You would also have to turn over the card bearing a picture of some keys. If this has an even number on the other side, then you know my claim is false.

You would *not* have to check the card with a 3 on it, because whatever is on the other side is irrelevant to my claim. The same applies to the card with a bear on it, because whatever is on the other side makes no difference to my claim.

Most people find they have to think this through very carefully before they realise the correct answer. A lot of people think it's important to check what's on the other side of the bear picture, but this isn't so. My claim is 'Every card that has an even number on one side has a picture of a bear on the other side.' My claim is *not*, 'Every card that has a bear on one side has an even number on the other side'.

This famous logic puzzle is known as the Wason Selection Task and you can read more about it online if you want to.

Gilan's Persuasion Tips

Here are three simple tips for you based on this chapter:

- Understand the role that intuition can play in your own decisions, and those that other people make. Triggering someone's System 1 intuitive thinking can often give you a persuasive advantage.

- Hone your own intuition, and remember that you have to be in a good mood or a happy state of mind for your intuition to work best!

- Be aware of the pitfalls of intuitive thinking, and how factors such as 'availability' heuristics can sometimes lead you astray if you're not careful.

Summary

In this chapter we looked at two kinds of intuition.

The first was 'sixth sense' intuition, where a great deal of experience in a particular field leads to what seems like an uncanny level of intuitive wisdom.

The second was 'speed reasoning' intuition, which we divided into 'substitution' heuristics and 'availability' heuristics. We saw how the effect of both these heuristics is amplified by the familiar phenomenon of egocentric bias.

The next chapter is about a very specific set of persuasion strategies. To start the chapter, I'm going to do something I very rarely do. I'm going to reveal one of my mindreading secrets…

A Small, Simple Favour

Will you do something very simple for me?

Because it's important.

I sincerely hope you are enjoying this book and getting some value from it. I'd like you to do me one, small favour. It involves very little time or effort, won't cost you anything, and is a *very* kind and helpful thing to do.

Please just tell other people about this book.

That's it! Everyone knows the best form of advertising is 'word of mouth', so I'm asking you to tell your friends and colleagues about my book.

I bet you have an email list of friends and contacts. Why not send out a group email about this book and some of the ideas it contains?

You could also post (favourable) messages on social media websites and online forums.

That's all I ask. It's easy to do, it will help me enormously, and I will be genuinely grateful.

THANK YOU!

Gilan Gork

www.gilangork.com

9: Mind Writing

"I think the power of persuasion would be the greatest superpower of all time."

— *Jenny Mollen*

A Special Secret

Here's a story that I tell a hundred times every year.

There's a cocktail party, and it's all going well. People are enjoying themselves, mixing and mingling, having a good time. One of the men at the party sits down at the piano and starts to play some beautiful jazz tunes. It's smooth, rhythmic, beautiful music that lifts the mood and enchants everyone present. What's more, it's clear that the piano player is doing this rather effortlessly. He barely seems to even look at the keys, yet this beautiful music continues to fill the room. Another guy leans over and says, 'Gee, I'd love to be able to play the piano like you.' Without missing a beat, the piano player says, 'Would you also like to have practised every day for twenty years, like I've had to do?'

When people see me reading minds, they often say they'd like to be able to do the same sort of thing. That's when I trot out the piano story. It's not that I mean to be unkind or impolite. It's just that when people say they'd like to be able to do what I do, that's not what they really mean. What they mean is they'd like to be able to do what I do so long as it's *easy* and they can learn it all *quickly*.

This is another reason why I tend not to talk much about how I do what I do. Some people think I have some sort of obsessive need to keep 'secrets'. Actually, this has never been a major compulsion with me. Quite honestly, the main reason is this: it would take me a very long time to explain, you'd probably get bored after the first hour or so of detailed explanation, and even then you wouldn't be able to do the same stuff because you'd have to practise. When I say you'd have to practise, I don't mean for a few years. I mean for a *decade* or more. You may think I'm kidding about this. Believe me — I wish that I were.

However, in this chapter I *am* going to share a secret with you. It's the method behind a small percentage of what I do, and it's one that very few people ever guess or figure out. Ready?

A lot of the time, when it looks like I'm reading someone's mind, I'm actually doing the opposite. I am not taking thoughts *out*, I'm putting thoughts *in*. There are several ways to do this, as we will see in this chapter. I won't be discussing the specific methods that I use in my work, since you don't have to do the same, strange things as me. Instead, I want to look at these methods in more general terms that may apply to your social or professional life, or any context where persuasion games are played.

Priming

We all cling to the fond notion that we are autonomous agents, completely in control of our thoughts and actions. While this may be true some of the time, I can positively guarantee it isn't true *all* of the time. The slightly unpalatable truth is that both your actions and emotions can be driven by external factors, including ones that you may not even know about. In general terms, this is called priming.

One example of priming applied to actions is the 'ideomotor' effect or response. You can prove this works whenever you want. Tie a key to the end of a piece of cotton thread about 20 centimetres long. This is now a pendulum.

Ask a friend to hold this by pinching the loose end between his forefinger and thumb, with his arm more or less outstretched. The key is allowed to swing freely. Tell him that the pendulum has been scientifically proved to be able to tell truth from lies. Tell him that when he makes a true statement, it tends to swing in a back and forth motion (or sometimes side to side), but when he makes a false statement it tends to swing in a circle. You may like to mention in passing that this works best with smart, intelligent people who can concentrate pretty clearly.

Let your friend say something that is obviously true, such as, 'My name is…' and he adds his own name. Then let him say something that is obviously untrue, such as 'I live in…' and he mentions a place that he has never ever visited, on the other side of the world. He will find, to his great delight, that the pendulum responds appropriately every time.

This demonstration won't work on people who are very cynical or who have read about the ideomotor effect before. However, it works on pretty much everyone else. The pendulum doesn't actually know anything. The only reason it swings back and forth, or in a circle, is because you've told your friend that that's what it does. Their own very subtle movements affect the key on the thread and make it swing the way you *primed* them to *expect* it to swing. If you prime someone else the opposite way (circle for true, back and forth for false), they'll find that's what the pendulum does.

Curiously knowledgeable pendulums can be a fun party trick to share, but this is actually quite a deep and interesting subject. Plenty of research has shown that priming can operate at quite subtle and delicate levels.

For example, psychologist John Bargh discovered a form of priming that he referred to as The Florida Effect. In the United States, the state of Florida is often associated with people of retirement age and retirement communities. Bargh conducted an experiment on some young university students. He gave them a set of five words and asked them to use any four of them to create a simple sentence. For example, the students were given, 'Daily Home Cycled He Light', from which it's possible to create the sentence, 'He cycled home daily'. Half the students were given sentences that had some connection with the elderly such as 'grey', 'wrinkled', 'aged' and 'Florida'.

After they had completed a series of these tasks, the students were asked to walk down a short corridor to their next task. The students who had been primed to think of the elderly walked to their next task *far more slowly* than those in the other group!

The subtle priming actually produced two related effects: the students thought of old age even if the word 'old' was never mentioned, and their behaviour was altered (walking more slowly). The students were subsequently interviewed about the experiment. All of them said they were completely unaware of any particular theme in the 'five words' task, and felt sure it couldn't have influenced their actions or behaviour afterwards. This is a very clear illustration of the ideomotor effect: a change in behaviour due to priming that the subject is completely unaware of.

As well as physical actions, priming can also affect emotions. The work of Freud and Jung provided us with many insights into the role of symbols and metaphors in unconscious associations. While some of their work may now be open to question, or at least refinement, there is no doubt that priming can affect feelings and perception.

This has been demonstrated scientifically. Researchers asked groups of volunteers to complete words with missing letters, like this:

W _ _ H

S _ _ P

Some volunteers were not primed in any way. They tended to suggest words like 'Wish' and 'Soup'. Other volunteers were primed by first of all asking them to think of anything they had ever done that they were ashamed of, or that they knew they shouldn't have done. These volunteers were more likely to think of words like 'Wash' and 'Soap'.

Psychologists refer to this as the Lady Macbeth effect (after the Shakespearean character whose guilt causes her to walk in her sleep and try to cleanse imaginary bloodstains from her hands). The 'cleansing' we choose can even show what type of shameful or bad thoughts we are thinking. In a different study, volunteers were asked to lie to a research assistant either over the phone or by email. The volunteers were then asked to rate the desirability of certain products. Those who lied by email were drawn towards soap while those who lied over the phone preferred mouthwash.

Suggestion

I know two things about the subject of priming by suggestion. The first is that it's a terribly simple subject. The second is that it is anything but a simple subject, and you could probably study it for a lifetime and not even scratch the surface.

The simple part goes like this: when you suggest things to people, you can affect what they see, hear and perceive. If you want to prove this, wait until the next time you're with a group of people and allow yourself to enjoy a large, satisfying yawn. Many of those you're with will feel the need to yawn as well. They may stifle the response, but you'll be able to tell that they felt like yawning. (And quite a few of you will have felt like yawning now, just by reading this paragraph!)

This just goes to show that the suggestion doesn't always have to be verbal. You can 'suggest' something to someone in lots of ways: words, sounds, gestures, expressions, actions and so on.

However, there's a lot more to suggestion than this, and the research into this fascinating field goes on and on for ever. This may be because it's an endlessly absorbing subject, or because research psychologists love seeing how they can 'suggest' things to people to mislead them.

In one experiment, a psychologist asked volunteers to sit in rows facing a table on which he had placed a small bottle of green liquid. He opened the bottle, and asked the volunteers to raise their hand when they could detect the peppermint smell of the liquid as it permeated the room. Not only did most of the volunteers indicate that they could detect the distinctive peppermint aroma, but some near the front said the smell was so overpowering they needed to leave the room. The green liquid was in fact just water plus green colouring. There was no peppermint smell, except in the imagination of the volunteers.

Sensory scientist Michael O'Mahoney created a new version of this experiment in the late 1970s when he broadcast a sound that he said would evoke a 'fresh, country smell'. British entertainer Derren Brown used the same idea in his TV show, 'Fear and Faith'. A search for #derrensmells on Twitter will show just how many people fell for the power of suggestion.

Suggestion plays a part in cold reading, but only a relatively minor one. For example, the psychic can say something like, 'There's an indication that a few problems and negative influences have been on your mind, but more recently you've been feeling a little more confident and have formed a few ideas about how to deal with them.' The very act of suggesting that this is what the client has been feeling recently could, in many cases, be enough to make the client feel that yes, this is exactly how she *has* been feeling. Such are the wonders and scintillating delights of the psychic world.

Suggestion has an even greater part to play in the world of psychic healing. The placebo effect is well documented. The very act of telling someone that a tablet is likely to alleviate their symptoms is enough, in many cases, to either (a) make the patient feel that their condition is improving (even when it isn't) or (b) to *actually* bring about some improvement. I will return to the subject of placebos later in Chapter 10.

Healing Words

When it comes to psychic healing, there's more to suggestion than just the placebo effect. The fact is, pain and discomfort are wholly subjective. Even today, with all the wonderful advances in medical science, there is no reliable, objective way to detect or measure pain. All a doctor can do is ask the patient to assess his level of pain himself, sometimes aided by a 'scale' to guide the assessment (e.g. 0 = no pain at all, 10 = as much pain as it's possible to imagine).

This is why there's often a lot of controversy attached to insurance claims. Someone who has been involved in a minor accident can tell his doctor he has been suffering severe back pain ever since, and get a doctor's report that would seem to justify a very high compensation payment. However, it may be a bogus claim from someone just hoping for a big pile of money. The doctor can't tell, despite all his qualifications and expertise. All he can do is ask the claimant, 'How much pain do you feel?'

It's the same in the world of psychic healing. The healer may say to his patient, 'I'm going to send some healing energy through, and this will make the pain less intense and more bearable.' What's likely to happen in a case like this? Well, let's look at the facts.

(1) The patient is evidently very keen to obtain some pain relief, or else he wouldn't have bothered to seek out the healer.

(2) The patient believes that the healer can help, or at least that this is a *possibility* (or else he wouldn't be there).

(3) The patient doesn't want to feel a complete fool for having come all this way to see a healer who is useless.

Given that the experience of pain is always at least partially subjective, the patient can always manage to convince himself that, yes, actually, his pain *does* now seem a bit less intense and more manageable.

Incidentally, I am not decrying this phenomenon or debunking it as a useless mind trick. I'm all in favour of people suffering as little pain in this life as possible, and if a very convincing suggestion from a healer helps them to perceive less pain, that's great. The problems only arise when the healer starts telling the patient nonsensical and dangerous things like, 'You must *only* come to me, only receive *my* treatment, and ignore whatever your doctor and conventional medicine tells you.' This kind of thing is very dangerous and should be opposed at every turn. Fortunately, it's quite rare, and most healers are neither so dangerous nor so stupidly irresponsible. The majority advise their patients to take whatever treatment their doctor prescribes, and to use their own 'healing' services to complement conventional medicine rather than to replace it.

Anchoring

Anchoring is a distortion of your ability to estimate values. It works by simply supplying numbers and values that influence your estimation, even though you don't realise it.

Here's an experiment you can try for yourself. Ask a few friends to estimate how many people live in Australia. For one group of friends, say, 'I'll tell you the correct answer is between 20 million and 40 million.' For the second group, say, 'I'll tell you the correct answer is between 10 million and 25 million'.

The correct total, at least at the time of writing this book, is a little more than 23-million. Of course, it's hard to get an accurate figure since on any given day, about five thousand Australians are slaughtered by gigantic killer spiders that attack people and drag them off to their lairs, kicking and screaming, never to be heard from again. (This is scientific fact.)

Back to the experiment. Most of your friends in the first group will give a pretty high population estimate, while most of those in the second group will give a pretty low estimate. Why? Because you supplied some numbers that interfered with their ability to come up with a good estimate. (By the way, in this era of widespread online social media, you can conduct your own research into anchoring very easily. Contact twenty friends online and ask them the first version of the question, then contact twenty different friends and ask them the second version. Of course, this process requires you to have forty online friends. If you haven't got this many friends, you may want to think about going to Australia? They're all *very* friendly people.)

Wine Trade

You can find examples of anchoring all around you. Suppose you run a restaurant and you'd like to sell a particular wine for amount X, even though it's quite a high price and not very good value. One way to do this is to put it on a list with several other wines listed above it at a significantly higher price, and some other listed below it at a very cheap price. A lot of people will think to themselves, 'I don't want to go crazy and spend a small fortune on what is, after all, just a bottle of wine; but then again, I don't want one of these cheap, nasty wines at the bottom that will probably taste like vinegar strained through an old sock. I'll compromise and go for this reasonable wine in the middle.'

A note of clarification: the social sciences do not always offer neat and universally agreed terminology. What I am here describing as 'anchoring' is, in other places, referred to as 'framing', whereas my own version of 'framing' is coming up in a few pages. Don't worry about this. I'm sharing a few ideas about persuasion, not trying to write a dictionary that the whole world will agree on. It's the ideas that matter, not the names. That having been said, you may wish to make life a lot simpler for yourself by taking the view that all other sources are always wrong and I'm always correct. I don't say you *ought* to take this view, but I'm just pointing out that you *can* and I'd admire you for it if you did.

Researchers can not only demonstrate that anchoring works, but they can also measure it. In Kevin Dutton's book 'Flipnosis', he supplies another example. Researchers asked people, 'How much jet fuel do you think it takes to fill a jumbo jet? Would you say more, or less, than 50,000 litres?' They then asked the same question but used '500,000 litres' as the anchor value. By comparing the average answers from these two surveys, researchers were able to calculate the difference between them, and found that the second group gave significantly higher estimates. The correct answer is about 220,000 litres.

Anyone selling houses knows all about anchoring. The same house will appear more valuable if its listing price is high than if it is low, and this will influence whether you want to buy it or not. Interestingly, anchoring doesn't just work on the people that estate agents deal with — it also works on estate agents.

In an experiment conducted some years ago, professional estate agents were given the opportunity to assess the value of a house that was on the market. They visited the house and studied a comprehensive booklet of information that included an asking price. Half the agents were given an asking price substantially higher than the listed price of the house, while the other half were given one substantially lower. Each agent gave their opinion as to a reasonable buying price and the lowest price they'd sell at if they owned the house. The difference was 41%. Interestingly, when asked about which factors had affected their judgement, they took pride in claiming they had *ignored* the asking price in the brochure.

Anchored Readings

You will not be surprised to learn that anchoring can play a part in the art of cold reading. In fact, one cold reader I know told me a story in which he not only used anchoring to make his own reading seem pretty accurate, but also to make his client feel pretty good about her prospects. It went something like this. The cold reader said, 'Your money line seems to indicate that you might run into quite a lot of money in the future... .' Before he could go any further, his client said, 'Well I'm not sure how, because I'm getting no inheritance and I'm studying to be a teacher — which pays very little!'. The psychic saw the perfect opportunity for anchoring and said, 'Well, maybe so, but how many teachers would you say marry wealthy men? Do you think it's more than 75% or less?'

The true figure for how many teachers end up marrying into wealth is probably quite low, but by using the anchor value of 75%, the reader was skewing his client's estimation, and hoping she would suggest any figure greater than 50%. Sure enough, in this case the client thought for a moment and suggested a figure that was greater than 50%. The cold reader smiled and said, 'Well, then we agree that you have a higher than average chance of marrying into some money!' Thus the statement was accepted as both true and insightful.

Of course, the anchoring might *not* have worked, and the client might have mentioned a figure below 50%. If this has happened, the psychic would just have said something else. For example, 'I'm not so sure. I think it's probably way more than 50%. In any case, the cards are clearly indicating some wealth so you've got luck and destiny on your side! Besides, don't you feel that you've worked hard and you *deserve* some success and prosperity?' The client agrees, and the cold reader says, 'Well, there you go then, it's likely to come true.' In the wonderful world of cold reading, the psychic is always right in the end.

Selling Skills

Anchoring also plays a part in what are known as 'single-issue' negotiations, meaning that there is only one issue to be settled between buyer and seller (such as price). As in many games, the person who makes the first bid or offer has the advantage, because this figure becomes an anchor for the negotiation. If the first figure mentioned is 100, the negotiation becomes about how much higher or lower than 100 the price should be. If the first figure mentioned is 200, it becomes about how much higher or lower than 200 it ought to be. You can appreciate that this makes a significant difference to the conversation!

We are all susceptible to the powerful and sometimes corrosive influence of anchoring. It works so well because it affects our System 1 thinking, and therefore can affect us at a subconscious level.

In a retail setting, the retailer might use an anchoring principle known as 'arbitrary rationing'. A few years ago, supermarket shoppers in Sioux City, Iowa, saw a sales promotion for Campbell's soup, which was being offered at 10% below the regular price. On some days, a sign on the shelf said, 'Limit of 12 per person'. On other days, there was no stipulated limit. Shoppers purchased an average of seven cans of soup when there was a stated limit, twice as many as they bought when the limit was removed. The prominent mention of the number 12 produced an anchoring effect.

This example is actually quite interesting since there is more than just anchoring involved. Rationing implies that the goods are very popular and flying off the shelves, and shoppers should feel some urgency about stocking up in case they miss out. Hence there are several factors involved such as social proof, scarcity, fear of missing out and framing (we will come to framing later in this chapter).

Coherence and Contrast

The anchoring principle leads to a related effect with the delightful name of arbitrary coherence. It works like this. Suppose I tell you what I think is a reasonable price to pay for a bottle of 12-year-old malt whisky. This figure will affect what you would expect to pay for a bottle of 15-year-old whisky. Even if the first figure was fairly arbitrary, you can't help using it when you calculate what the second figure should be. Your mind naturally craves some coherence between the two figures.

In the world of cold reading, this same desire for coherence plays its part in the perceived accuracy of many predictions. Consider the case of someone with a mild belief in psychic powers. The psychic reads the cards, tea leaves or whatever, and offers some seemingly accurate statements about the client's present situation followed by some predictions for the future. If the client accepts the statements about her present circumstances, she will form a *coherent* expectation that the predictions will also turn out to be fairly accurate. She will be prone to notice anything that matches the predictions, or can be interpreted to match them, and to conveniently forget anything that doesn't fit.

One reason for this intriguing phenomenon is that to the mind, everything is relative. You rarely have the resources to evaluate things in absolute terms. The best you can do is relate one value to another. If I ask you to guess someone's precise age, you'd find it difficult to offer anything other than a reasonable guess. On the other hand, if I ask you to say whether Person A is older or younger than Person B, you'd probably come up with the correct answer in 99% of cases.

Our sensitivity to the contrast between two values or experiences can mislead us. Line up three buckets: one contains hot water, one contains cold water, and the middle bucket is at room temperature. Put your left hand in the hot water and your right hand in the cold water for 20 seconds, and then put both into the middle bucket. Your left hand will tell you the water is rather cold, while your right hand will tell you the water is rather hot.

Three Boxes

If you want, you can experience the most wonderful demonstration of this phenomenon for yourself. You need three identical boxes: two quite light and one relatively heavy. Two empty matchboxes and one filled with coins or weights will suffice for your first try (see picture 1).

Stack them as shown (2), with the one heavy box at the top. Using an overhand grip, grasp all three boxes from above and lift them an inch or two off the table (3). Put them down again.

Now just lift the top box on its own (4). Your brain will tell you that the top box, on its own, weighs more than all three boxes did when you lifted them together! This is clearly impossible.

Why does this work? In simple terms, your mind expects all three boxes to weigh the same because they are identical in appearance and it's simpler to assume coherence than to expect two light boxes and one heavy box. When you pick up the heavy box on its own, your brain is expecting to feel one-third of the combined weight, but actually experience much more than one-third. This gives rise to the confused sensation of 'greater heaviness than expected', and by extension the illusion that one box weighs more than all three did.

Contrast and Cold Reading

In cold reading, the fact that we pay more attention to contrast than to absolute values allows the reader to offer mild criticisms without giving offence.

For example, if the psychic were to say, 'You have a selfish streak', the client would probably reject this assessment and feel rather insulted. However, the psychic can use contrast to make the statement more palatable, like this: 'We all know the type of person who is completely self-absorbed and doesn't give much time to anyone else... yes? You can probably think of someone like that in your life. Well, I sense that you are not like that at all. In fact, you are generally very selfless and you do a lot for other people. Mind you, if you're very honest, I think you can accept that on rare occasions you can act a little selfishly, even if this isn't really in your nature.' It's basically the same message, but the second version is much more acceptable than the first because it is expressed in comparative terms, not absolutely ones.

You may wonder why a cold reader would *want* to offer mild criticisms, rather than just saying nice, flattering things all the time. Well, not all do. There are some readers who will indeed just spout lots of flattering nonsense in the hope of getting some repeat trade — a strategy that has been known to work in the past.

However, given that the reading is supposed to be delivering some insight mixed with a little wisdom and advice, the 'Everything about you is great, all the time' approach would sound false and also offer very little for the psychic to do. The 'You're basically great but with just a few minor faults you could work on' approach sounds far more plausible, and allows the psychic to play the wise counsellor.

The principle of contrasts also affects the way retail clothing stores train their sales staff. They always strive to sell the more expensive items first. Once a customer has bought something expensive, the less expensive items start to look like really good bargains, even if they are still fairly costly in absolute terms. This is especially true for accessories. Sales motivation analysts Whitney, Hubin and Murphey write:

> "The interesting thing is that even when a man enters a clothing store with the express purpose of purchasing a suit, he will almost always pay more for whatever accessories he buys if he buys them after the suit purchase than before."

Holiday Choices

Here's another interesting example of persuasion games based on contrast. Suppose I run a travel company, and I offer you two comparable holiday trips: one to Venice and the other to Monte Carlo. The two trips offer similar activities and value for money, and in both cases all the costs are included. If I'd prefer you to choose Venice, because it's more profitable for my company, what should I do?

One good strategy would be to introduce a third holiday option, also to Venice, and make it a cheaper holiday but with some costs *not* included (such as airport taxes or meals). I could make it easy to see that this decoy option offers less value for money than the first Venice option. In this situation, most people would focus on the two Venice options (because they can be compared), correctly deduce that the first one offers better value for money, and purchase it. The Monte Carlo option would get overlooked, because there's no comparison involved.

Framing

The way that information is presented to you can affect your instinctive feelings about it, leading to the formation of 'empty intuitions'. This is known as framing. It can lead to the embarrassingly familiar situation in which you feel quite strongly about something even though it subsequently turns out that you're wrong. You will not be surprised to hear that research psychologists have studied this in some detail. They just *love* devising experiments in which sweet, innocent people are lured into making idiots of themselves. Here's an example.

Imagine that the United States is preparing for the outbreak of an unusual disease that is expected to kill about 600 people. There are two alternative programmes to combat the disease. If programme A is adopted, 200 people will be saved. If programme B is adopted, there is a one-third probability that 600 people will be saved and a two-thirds probability that no people will be saved. Which programme would you choose to implement? A substantial majority of respondents choose programme A, saying they prefer the certain benefit to the gamble. So far, so good.

The projected outcomes of the two programmes are framed differently in a second version. If programme A is adopted, 400 people will die. If programme B is adopted, there is a one-third probability that nobody will die and a two-thirds probability that 600 people will die. When the programmes are presented in this way, a large majority of people choose programme B. The preference has changed, even though the projected outcomes in both cases are identical.

Similar examples arise in other contexts, such as legal cases. Consider the example of an attorney who wants to persuade the jury that some DNA evidence is unreliable. He will not say, 'The chance of a false match is 0.1%'. He would be more likely to say something like, 'A false match occurs in 1 of 1000 capital cases', which is far more likely to be considered 'a reasonable doubt'. The careful wording makes all the difference.

Framed Readings

Framing crops up a lot in cold reading. To see how it works, consider a psychic who says something like this: 'I'm not sure what to say, or what this means. It's all a bit vague to me and I don't really have anything specific to tell you.' Even by the desperately low standards of the cold reading industry, where a good guess is on a par with profound psychic powers, I suspect this would be regarded as a poor show, neither helpful nor impressive. However, suppose the psychic kicks off the reading with this sort of introduction: 'Let me advise you that in many cases, the impressions I get might make more sense to you than to me. Sometimes, there is some degree of interpretation needed if you want to get the most from the reading. We can work on this together.' With this framing, any vagueness or lack of precise expression seems like a *validation* of the psychic process rather than a fault with it.

Another beautiful example of framing, or reframing, has to do with how psychics ask questions and prompt for feedback *while apparently doing neither*. If the psychic says, 'There are indications that you're thinking of getting a new job... am I right about this?', then it doesn't sound very psychic. It sounds like someone making a guess and then asking if it happens to be correct — which is exactly what's going on.

Now consider this example: 'There are indications that you're thinking of getting a new job... how might you relate to this?' Now it *sounds* as if the psychic is making a definite statement, and then — almost as an afterthought — wondering what the client can add in terms of fine tuning and small details. The two statements are identical except for the framing.

Framing the Fails

Framing can also transform apparent failure into something else. Consider a psychic who has a favourite party piece, such as offering you a choice from four or five picture cards and guessing which one you've chosen. If he guesses and fails, there's little to be salvaged from the episode except to note that he failed.

However, suppose he offers a little introduction and says, 'A lot of people say that the sorts of things I do must be a trick, like a magic trick. But that's not true. Magic tricks work every time, whereas my gift can vary. Some days I feel great and it works very well, whereas at other times I feel a little tired and things don't work the way I want them to.'

Given this framing, any demonstration that ends in failure does not equate to 'He's not a very good psychic', but to 'At least we know it's not some sort of trick, because if it were, it would work every time'. Paradoxically, the 'failure' comes to be seen as further proof that the psychic's powers are real. Such is the majestic power of shrewd framing.

Framing crops up in countless areas of life. What does the government (any government) say about economic news? If the news happens to be good, they say, 'This news is a direct result of our policies and shows we're on the right track.' If the news happens to be bad, they say, 'This news is a result of a general downturn in the global economy, and other factors that have nothing to do with us.'

An advertising company produces a campaign for an existing product. If sales improve, the ad agency says, 'This is a direct result of our very clever, successful campaign.' If sales go down, the agency says, 'Sales would have gone down a lot further without our clever, successful campaign.'

You can probably think of other examples.

Sequence

A strategy related to framing has to do with the sequence in which you present information.

American author Frank Luntz, an expert on political polling in the United States, once conducted a focus group to test different TV adverts for Ross Perot, who was running for president at the time. One of the adverts was basically just Perot giving a speech, the second contained a series of testimonials and endorsements, and the third was essentially a potted biography of the candidate.

Luntz found that he got different results depending on the order in which he showed these possible adverts. If he showed them in biography / speech / testimonials order, the focus group's responses, including how likely they would be to vote for Perot, was very similar to other polls, including national polls that tracked how Perot was doing. However, if he played the adverts in a different order, saving the biographical advert until last, far *fewer* members of the focus group said they would vote for him. Only the order of the adverts had changed. It seemed that unless people knew about Perot's history, his speeches came across as unreasonable and excessive. Luntz concluded that the order in which information is presented can determine how people think, and may be just as important as the actual content.

I often have cause to think about sequencing because of a recurring problem. Professionally, I do a few different things and wear a few different hats. When I meet a new business contact for the first time, in what order should I mention the things I do?

If I say I read minds, they think I have my head in the clouds (or somewhere even worse) and I can't possibly have anything useful to say about serious business matters.

If I say I am a corporate speaker and trainer, they may stereotype me as either a 'death-by-Powerpoint' specialist or, at the other extreme, a 'Rah rah rah! Go for it!' motivational speaker. I don't know which of these is worse, but I try to be neither.

If I say I am an entertainer, they don't take me seriously as a conference speaker and trainer.

However, I have found this sequence to be quite successful:

1. I'm a mentalist (their response: 'Oh what's that?')

2. Well, basically, I teach you how to read and influence people…

3. …and I do this through either corporate talks and training, or by presenting mind-reading shows.

Poll Science

The world of surveys and public opinion polls is fascinating, and full of quirks. It has been known for a long time that the way you ask or phrase a question can often influence the answers you get, and sometimes the sequence in which questions are asked can also introduce distortions.

Suppose you are ostensibly sampling opinion about whether a new sports centre should be built in your neighbourhood — one that will eat up a lot of local expenditure. You can start with a few questions along these lines, 'Do you support providing young people with facilities to help their health and education and to keep them away from gangs, drugs and crime?' Then you can ask, 'Would you support the building of the new sports centre?' Most people will say yes.

Alternatively, you can start with some questions about the way councils waste money and spend vast sums on projects that lead nowhere, e.g. 'Do you support initiatives to rein in wasteful council spending and give taxpayers better value for money?' If you now ask about the sports centre, most people will say no.

Gilan's Persuasion Tips

Here are three simple tips for you based on this chapter:

- Use the power of priming to help you persuade successfully. In essence: tell people what's going to happen, and that's what they'll expect!

- Use anchoring so that people perceive numbers, values, prices and other figures the way *you* want them to.

- Use framing and sequencing to shape how people see your ideas or points, always remembering that good framing can even turn a failure into a qualified success.

Summary

In this chapter I started by revealing that mind-reading is sometimes more about 'mind writing'. This led to exploration of priming, anchoring and other ways of putting ideas into the minds of other people, and shaping their thoughts to suit your own purposes.

We also looked at the power of framing, and the related concept of sequencing information in whatever way best suits your persuasive goals.

In the next chapter, we will explore the intriguing relationship between expectations and experience. This will lead us to one of the most fascinating and powerful persuasive phenomena in the world: the placebo effect.

10: Managing Expectations

"The mind is no match with the heart in persuasion; constitutionality is no match with compassion."

— *Everett Dirksen*

Creating Belief

Let's say I want to sell you a car. There are several things I can do to try to persuade you to buy the car, but there's one thing I can do that's more effective than anything else. Do you know what it is?

I can smarten up my appearance, make sure my hair is neat, my breath is fresh and my hands (and fingernails) are clean, and generally try to be the most pleasant and likeable version of me I can be.

I can be a good listener, and make sure I understand your needs, wants and aspirations as a customer, and then try to shape my sales pitch accordingly, trying to show the correspondence between what you want and what this car offers.

I can use what's called SPIN selling, and structure my pitch around *situation, problem, implication* and *need/payoff* questions. (If you're interested in this very interesting sales strategy, check out the work of Neil Rackham.)

I can use any one of dozens of other sales strategies that people have devised over the years, many of them with catchy acronyms that look good on the cover of a business book at the airport.

I can try to build 'yes sets', getting your agreement on a series of small details so it's easier to get your agreement on larger ones (such as actually buying the car).

All of these ideas and strategies have their merits. However, there's one thing I can do that is more effective than any of these: I can get you to *believe* that you want and need the car. If you believe that, then I really have to do very little selling at all. I just have to smile nicely, sit you down and fetch the paperwork.

So far, so good. But how can I create this belief in you? I don't own a magic ray gun that I can aim at your head to create whatever belief I want. However, I can use a few strategies that help to create belief, and — by extension — create the *consequences* of belief. That's what this chapter is all about.

Forming Expectations

You are forming expectations all the time. This is a good thing, because it's essential for your survival. You have learned to expect that if you spill a pan of boiling water all over yourself, it will hurt a lot and could lead to a permanent injury, so you take care to avoid doing it. Likewise with stepping out in front of a moving car, sticking your head into a hornet's nest or telling your spouse that his jokes are actually very tiresome or she's put on weight recently.

On the positive side, you have learned to give people as much honesty as you'd like to receive in return, to defer gratification and work steadily towards the completion of long-term projects, and to save some of your money for a rainy day. All of these behaviours involve being able to form an expectation of how current events are likely to play out in the future. Your brain forms expectations all the time, every day, partly because it likes to detect patterns (all expectations are based on patterns from past experience) and partly because it wants to survive and avoid dangerous surprises.

David Huron, in his book *Sweet Anticipation: Music and the Psychology of Expectation*, puts it like this:

> *'Forming expectations is what humans and other animals do to survive; only by predicting the future can we be ready for it. And because the brain ensures that accurate prediction is rewarded, we feel good when we are proved right. The link between prediction and reward causes us to constantly seek out structure and predict how events will unfold.'*

Unfortunately, your innate and constant tendency to form expectations can be exploited and used against you. You will know about this if you have ever purchased something on the basis of loyalty to a given person, celebrity, group, brand or reputation, only to discover that it wasn't very good. The hype machine exploited the wiring in your head, and now the movie studio has your money and you've wasted two hours of your life that you'll never get back. (The interesting thing about this example is that we all think we've learned this particular lesson, but we continue to fall for it anyway. This is the pernicious persistence of persuasive promotion, and yes, I made that phrase up all by myself. You're welcome.)

The Plausible Placebo

Earlier in this book, we looked at the power of suggestion and how people felt they could smell a rich minty aroma from a bottle containing nothing but water and dye. Part of the explanation is that the people involved in the experiment were expecting this particular aroma.

Your expectations don't just affect specific short-term sensations, such as how you perceive and interpret sights, sounds, tastes and other sensory data. They can also shape your subjective experience over a long time. Perhaps the most fascinating example is that of the placebo effect. The word 'placebo' (Latin for 'I shall please') was used in the fourteenth century to refer to sham mourners hired to wail and sob, in a rather histrionic manner, at funerals. By 1785 it appeared in the New Medical Dictionary, associated with marginal medicinal practices.

Let me explain the basic idea just in case you haven't come across this term before. Suppose you are a doctor, and you are treating a group of patients for a particular condition. You give them a particular pill, which medical research suggests delivers a particular benefit, and your patients report that they feel better and the pill helped to alleviate their symptoms. This sounds like a fairly simple case of cause and effect, doesn't it? Give pill to person, person feels better. Couldn't be simpler.

However, we now know that in many cases, you can give those patients a pill that is medically inert, with no active pharmaceutical ingredients whatsoever, and a significant percentage of the patients will report *exactly the same benefits*. I don't just mean they report that they feel better (which could be 'all in the mind'). I mean their actual symptoms respond just as they did when they took the 'real' pill that offers the best assistance medical science can devise.

Arterial Flaw

This remarkable effect has been the subject of countless research studies and ethical debates, and is still being studied in depth. Just to take one example. In 1939 an Italian surgeon named Fieschi devised a procedure to treat angina. He figured that if he could somehow increase blood flow to the patient's heart, this would ease the pain associated with angina. He achieved this by making tiny incisions and tying surgical knots in a few arteries. This procedure seemed to be remarkably effective. About three-quarters of patients said their condition improved, and as many as a third claimed they were cured altogether.

About twenty years later, the National Institutes of Health asked Dr Leonard A Cobb to test the Fieschi procedure in an interesting way. He operated on seventeen patients in all. In the case of eight patients, Dr Cobb copied the Fieschi procedure exactly — the same incisions, the same tying of knots in the arteries. In the case of the other nine patients, he just made the small incisions but didn't do anything else. In 1959, the *New England Journal of Medicine* reported that the fake operations, in which only incisions were made, were just as effective as the genuine operations. The Fieschi procedure, referred to as internal mammary artery ligation, fell out of favour and within a few years was relegated to a footnote in textbooks.

Price Perception

Research into the placebo effect has led to some interesting findings. For example, if patients are told the pill or treatment (actually a placebo) is very expensive, this works better than if they are told it's relatively cheap. Similarly, being told that the pill is quite rare and hard to get hold of works better than being told it is commonplace and widely available.

It's not hard to find other examples where perceived expense and rarity can affect conclusions and results. For example, Hilke Plassman, a researcher at the California Institute of Technology, wondered whether expectations could affect the taste and perceived quality of wine. She got an average bottle of Cabernet, and invited some participants to taste the wine and rate its quality. However, she told some tasters that it was a cheap $10 bottle of wine and others that it was worth $90. As you may guess, those who thought they were sampling an expensive wine offered much more favourable verdicts, and rated the wine very highly.

Horn Dilemma

The rather tragic market for aphrodisiacs involves several layers of warped expectations. Powdered rhino horn is believed to be a legitimate and effective aphrodisiac in many parts of the world. This is the first layer of mythology, since there is precisely zero evidence that rhino horn, whether powdered or not, has any aphrodisiac properties whatsoever. In fact, all the evidence we have suggests that there's only one good thing to do with a rhino horn, and that's to leave it on the front end of a rhinoceros. Unfortunately, the aphrodisiac myth leads to rhinos being hunted. This, in turn, leads to the rhino dying out in some places, and increased conservation efforts and protective security measures in others. Both of these factors mean that rhino horn becomes more scarce and hard to get hold of, which only intensifies the belief that it works and must be worth getting hold of. Hence the market price goes up, the poachers get offered even more money and increase their efforts. Poaching, conflict and bloodshed... for what? Something that doesn't work, can't work and has never worked. If you ever want a neat example of the madness of our species, there you have it.

Positive Belief

So, how does the placebo effect actually work? The truth is, we don't fully understand it. Your body has a tremendous ability to heal, cure and repair itself, but in some cases this 'self-healing' process simply fails to start, for reasons we don't understand. It seems that a placebo is somehow capable of 'triggering' the body's own amazing ability to heal and repair itself. That may seem like a fairly vague description, and it is. However, that's pretty much all we know.

Nonetheless, even though we may not know a lot about how or why placebos work, we can identify two of the mechanisms that seem to be involved in its operation and its efficacy: positive belief and conditioning.

If you sincerely believe something doesn't work then it very probably won't work for you, whereas if you sincerely believe something *does* work then in many cases it will — or at least it will *seem* to do so. The belief can be in the person administering the 'treatment', the procedure itself or the supposed 'drug'. It doesn't really matter.

Conditioning

You have a lot in common with a dog. It's true, and I'm not insulting you at all. Let me explain.

In the very early days of the twentieth century, Russian physiologist Ivan Pavlov was investigating the digestive systems of mammals, especially dogs. He noticed that whenever a plate of food was brought to the dog in his lab, the dog's salivary glands would start secreting saliva. However, he then noticed that the dog would also start secreting saliva when anything else happened that the dog associated with the arrival of food. For example, if the lab technician who normally provided the food walked into the room, the dog started producing saliva — even when the technician did not have any food, and it was not feeding time. The dog had not *learned* to salivate at feeding time.

140

This response seemed to be 'hard-wired', or autonomous. The same was true of the dog's response to anything associated with feeding. Pavlov devoted a large part of the rest of his life to studying this phenomenon. (His dog devoted a large part of the rest of his life to eating dog food and wondering why intelligent looking people kept watching him eat it.)

Pavlov was the first to study what is now referred to as classical conditioning — the process by which a given response (such as salivating) becomes linked with a given stimulus (such as the presence of a technician), even though the stimulus and response had no prior, necessary association.

Classical conditioning works on you, me and everyone else. If it didn't, there would be no such thing as branding. You order a pizza from a particular company, you enjoy the pizza and at some level you notice their distinctive colours and logo. Next time you walk down the street, you happen to see the company's logo and you start salivating much as you would as if you were just about to sample another of their wonderful pizzas. You can probably think of many other examples, and of course they don't all have to be about food and eating.

You watch a new TV show featuring a particular actor, and you find you really enjoy the show and find it gripping and entertaining. Next time you see that actor's name or picture, you experience some of that same sense of interest and excitement, even though you aren't watching TV and the actor is just featured in a press advert for life insurance. You have learned to associate a feeling and a response with a given stimulus, in a way which is *not* innate (i.e. there was a time when this association had *not* formed within you).

This type of conditioning clearly can play a part in placebo function. If you have learned to associate a given person, procedure or pill with a particular response (such as 'I now feel far less pain and less stiffness in my back') then you can experience the same response even if the pill is medically neutral and contains no active ingredients whatsoever.

Expectation Errors

The remarkable facility you have for forming associations and expectations can serve you very well, but it can also leave you susceptible to various persuasive strategies. A very common one is known as embroidering.

Imagine you need to hire a caterer. Company #1 offers 'delicious Asian-style ginger chicken' and 'flavourful Greek salad with kalamata olives and feta cheese'. Company #2 offers 'a sliver of scallop sashimi with lightly sweet Meyer lemon confit, crunchy toasted buckwheat kernels and tiny pieces of compressed apple, vacuum-packed to concentrate the flavour'.

Which would you choose? Most people would be inclined to hire company #2 just because the elaborate descriptions lead you to expect greater quality. This expectation is formed even though the two sets of descriptions tell you *nothing whatsoever* about the quality of the food or which company is offering better value.

We all tend to use this 'embroidering' strategy when it suits us. If you invite friends round to watch a movie, you may mention all the top stars in the movie, how many great reviews it has had, how many awards it has won and so on, all of which serves to create a positive expectation, which will be likely to increase everyone's enjoyment of the movie. I'm not suggesting this mechanism works perfectly or cannot be overridden by experience: we all know great expectations sometimes give way to dismay and disappointment. But we tend to play with our expectations, and those of our social circle, all the same.

Edification

Another strategy related to expectation errors is known as edifying or edification.

I learned a lot about this when I was still in my early twenties and running a network marketing team. Part of my job was to persuade people to join my team and stay with it. This experience taught me a great deal about different forms of influence and persuasion — the methods that work, and the ones that don't. For example, I soon learned that, 'I pay your salary, so do as I say' is a *very* poor persuasive strategy. People could choose to join my team, but they could choose to leave it just as quickly, and I had to always bear this in mind.

It didn't take me long to figure out that edification was a much better strategy. In simple terms, edifying someone means building them up, offering realistic praise at every opportunity, and saying good things about them to other people. Anyone can edify anyone else, and I found that trying to instil this as part of my company's culture paid huge dividends. It feels good if people are saying positive things about you, but it also feels good to be the person offering those positive views, opinions and reports.

An interesting aspect of edification is that the edification is more important than the source. You often see movie posters with favourable reviews splashed across them in the largest, boldest lettering that will fit, e.g. 'Movie of the year! You must see this!'. The name of the reviewer is written in tiny print underneath, because it doesn't really matter. The value of the review lies in what is said, not who said it.

However, there is one golden rule: you can't edify *yourself*.

Imagine you are visiting a clinic for an operation, and you're a little nervous because it's rather a risky procedure. A man strides confidently into the room. He exclaims, 'You must me by patient! You look nervous — but don't you worry! I am Doctor Johnson! I am the best! I have won numerous awards and everyone knows I am one of the most confident and competent surgeons around. You're absolutely safe with me!' How would you feel about Dr Johnson's confidence in himself?

Imagine this slightly different scenario. You're back in the clinic and the cleaner enters the room, mopping the floor. He says, 'You must be Doctor Johnson's patient. You look nervous. Well, don't you worry! Doctor Johnson is the best! He has won numerous awards and everyone knows that he's one of the most confident and competent surgeons around. You're absolutely safe with him!'

See the difference? You would feel much more confident about the doctor's abilities when the edification comes from a third party — even a humble cleaner!

I applied this thinking to my network marketing team in several different ways. For example, suppose that a member of my team was about to present a business plan to a group of prospects. I made sure we always used an edifying introduction script to raise the expectations in the room and increase the perceived value of whatever my team member was about to say. This worked very well, and certainly helped to encourage more people to sign up my team and our business plans.

Surprise and Shift

As we have seen, you are constantly searching for patterns and forming expectations based on past experience. In effect, you are constantly building a model of reality as you understand it. This *cognitive model* is something you carry around with you all the time. It represents your best understanding of how the world works, and can be *expected* to work in future.

Any experience you have can contribute to the model, but you will attach more significance to events and actions that happen with some regularity. The more consistent a particular sequence or pattern seems to be, the greater your expectation will be that you can predict future events. If you only ever see one piece of toast dropped once on the floor, you won't form any strong expectations about dropped toast. After a few more years of life experience, you come to realise the indisputable scientific fact that it always lands butter side down, and you form the expectation that this will always be the case. This expectation will always accord with reality.

If you did not carry this cognitive model of the world around with you in your head, you would be incapable of ever feeling surprised by anything. The experience of feeling surprised is both an indication that you have a mental model of how the world works and that this model is either flawed (you would have expected X but you got Y), or at least incomplete (you had no experience of either X or Y).

When you experience something for the first time, it may come as a considerable surprise. When you have the same experience again, it feels less surprising. Over time, you revise and update your mental model of the world to accommodate this experience, so it shifts from being considered 'surprising' to being considered 'normal'. This shift can happen almost imperceptibly, as your mind absorbs new data, extracts a pattern and forms new or refreshed expectations about what constitutes reality and normality.

Surprising Psychics

This process occurs all the time in the world of cold reading. It is not uncommon for a client, when visiting a psychic for the first time, to have a fairly neutral attitude — no strong belief, no strong disbelief. The psychic goes through the usual preamble and then makes a statement that seems broadly correct, if you allow a little latitude for interpretation. She says a few more things, and then gets another hit or partial hit. Each time this happens, the client will shift from 'no opinion either way' to 'this person is psychic and can make accurate statements about my life'. In other words, the belief is formed little by little, quite possibly without the client being aware that this is happening. The psychic seduction process can be very stealthy indeed.

This subtle shift from 'surprise' to 'normal' also has a bearing on the cold reader's ability to make statements about the future. There are many different ways in which cold readers can predict the future. One very reliable strategy is to include prophecies that have the delightful property of being self-fulfilling. In other words, they come true because you've been told they are going to come true. This is not difficult to do.

Consider a situation where the cold reader has already won the trust of the client. The reader says, 'There are indications here that your social life may have taken a bit of a back seat lately. Because of other preoccupations, you haven't always been as sociable as you might have been, and you've allowed some social opportunities to slip by. However, there are clear indications that this is set to change. I see you adopting a rather more positive attitude, and being willing to try new things and meet new people, and overall this is going to be a good thing that leads to some good news.'

The client goes home, having heard — from a source that she *trusts and believes* — that she is going to start behaving in a more outgoing and sociable way. There is a very strong chance this will affect how she responds to the next few social invitations that come her way, and there you go: another successful miracle of psychic forecasting. If only stocks and shares were as easy to influence.

In a case like this, it's easy to see how the client's expectations about her own behaviour can be subtly massaged in a particular direction, leading to behavioural modification. The changed behaviour is seen as *vindicating* the prediction, when in fact it was *caused* by it.

Cognitive Strain

Another very common source of erroneous judgement is cognitive ease or strain. You tend to favour ideas and assessments that are very easily brought to mind, and be biased against those that are difficult to bring to mind. We touched on this before with the availability heuristic — it's easy to bring to mind the idea that spiders are nasty and dangerous because many sources constantly supply the words, images and tales to support this view, even though it is factually incorrect. It's harder to rationally assess the facts and realise that spiders pose very little threat indeed because the sources of this (factually correct) information tend not to be as prominent or as frequently met.

This phenomenon gives rise to the notion of *predictable* illusions. If you know that your society or culture makes it very easy to access concept A (even if it's factually awry), and very difficult to access concept B (even if it's correct), then you can be confident that a majority of people you meet within that society or culture will be biased in favour of concept A. This can sometimes lead to very regrettable beliefs (e.g. prejudice against certain groups) or harmless but bemusing ones (e.g. 'crazy' fads and trends that come and go from time to time).

One way to reenforce this phenomenon is frequent repetition. Your mental apparatus finds it hard to distinguish familiarity from truth. In one interesting experiment...

This is known as the 'exposure effect'. The more often you meet the same idea, the less resistance you have to it. In normal, everyday life, if nobody were trying to influence your thinking or bias your judgements, you would only encounter the same data over and over again if it were part of what you perceive as your external reality. You would see birds flying very often because that's what birds do, and so you would quickly form the expectation that birds tend to fly. Now, consider an advertising campaign devoted to the notion that 'Gork Chocolate Tastes Great!'. If you see this message often enough, supported by appealing images of beautiful young people and upbeat music, you might well start to absorb this as a true statement, or at least an idea with some truth to it. This process would occur even if Gork Chocolate was the most foul-tasting, disgustingly sickly confection ever inflicted on human taste buds.

You will not be shocked to learn that repetition plays a part in the effectiveness of cold reading.

For example, at the start of a reading, the psychic might say, 'Sometimes the impressions I get might make more sense to you than they do to me... like a song that's familiar and recognisable to you but not to me... can you relate to that?', and give a subtle head nod. The client nods and says, 'Yes', and there's clearly nothing about this to disagree with.

From this point on, the psychic can keep using the phrase 'Can you relate to that?' with the little head nod, and each time the conditioned response gets stronger and becomes more automatic — even when the psychic is just guessing or saying things that really don't make a whole lot of sense. The repetition in this case helps to build a conditioned response.

Also, the psychic might use the phrase 'I'm not asking you to try to make anything fit' several times during the reading, so this becomes an easy phrase for the client to remember and take away. Afterwards, the client might sincerely believe that the psychic never encouraged her to try to make anything fit, even though in fact she did this almost constantly. The repetition makes it easy to adopt one judgement (she wasn't asking me to try to make anything fit) and very hard to adopt another (actually, when you analyse the reading in cold, hard detail, she was constantly nudging and encouraging me to invent links between her statements and my life).

Gilan's Persuasion Tips

Here are three simple tips for you based on this chapter:

- Recognise that creating beliefs and expectations is one of the most potent persuasion strategies of all.

- Use the power of expectations to create experiences, and learn from the incredible phenomenon of the placebo.

- Be aware of the ways in which 'expectation formation' can go astray. Make sure you don't fall prey to these common thinking traps.

Summary

In this chapter we looked at the incredible power of expectations to create experience, and spent some time looking at the 'miracle' of the placebo effect. Although we may not have complete understanding of placebo treatments, we know enough to be able to derive some important lessons in the art of persuasion.

We also looked at the important role of positive belief, and conditioning — which is another way of saying we aren't all that different from Pavlov's dog.

In the next chapter, we'll look at compliance: how to get people to comply with your wishes, while making sure they can't do the same to you.

11: Compliance

"The power of a movement lies in the fact that it can indeed change the habits of people. This change is not the result of force but of dedication, of moral persuasion."

— *Steve Biko*

Do As I Say

If you're playing persuasion games, there are times when you want other people to comply with your wishes. I have some bad news and some good news about this. The bad news is that the open, direct approach, 'Please comply with my wishes', has historically proved to be remarkably ineffective. Strange as it may seem, it tends to provoke entirely the opposite response, and spurs people to resist your ideas with great force.

The good news is that there are some very neat strategies for winning compliance. The main ones we'll be looking at in this chapter are social proof, authority, likeability, reciprocation and commitment.

I won't say they all work perfectly, all the time. I will say can all be remarkably effective when used appropriately.

Social Proof

Your brain uses whatever cues and clues it can to build your cognitive model of the world and everything in it. Of course, your own direct, personal experience of the world is a major source of information. However, you share the planet with a few billion other people, and your brain also likes to use their knowledge and experiences too.

This can be a perfectly sensible thing to do. It saves you having to figure out all of human civilisation for yourself. You don't need to work out how to make bread, beer or bath taps because someone else has done it for you.

The problem arises when you start to think that if lots of people believe something, it's probably true. This is referred to as the 'social proof' argument, also sometimes ironically termed 'the wisdom of crowds'.

There are at least two problems with social proof. The first is that lots of people are perfectly capable of believing things that aren't true, and the second is that popular opinion is very easily manipulated for commercial or political purposes. The 'wisdom of crowds' is very often little more than the hopelessly misguided opinion of crowds.

This was clearly demonstrated in one of the most famous experiments in psychology. Psychologist Solomon Asch showed students some slides featuring lines of various lengths. Asch asked each student in the group, one by one, to say which line was the longest. In actual fact, all the students except one were actors who said what Asch told them to say. During the first two or three slides, they all gave reasonable answers and nominated the longest line. As the experiment progressed, they started to nominate lines that were clearly *not* the longest. Asch found that in each set of students, the one person who was not an actor started going along with the group, and nominating lines that were clearly not the longest, despite the evidence of their own eyes.

It's rather alarming that we are all susceptible to this notion of 'social proof', and can change our beliefs and actions just to fit in with the crowd even in the face of clear contradictory evidence. We tend to suppose that if a great many people express the same belief, then it must have some basis in fact. What's more, the effect is self-propagating, in the sense that as more and more people adopt an idea, the easier it becomes for that idea to spread and to become an entrenched and unshakeable 'fact', even when it is entirely false.

I once attended a talk by holocaust survivor, Tomi Reichental, who came from a small town in Slovakia. When he was growing up, he told us, there was none of today's social media to spread the anti-Semitic propaganda of the Nazis. Instead, it was the churches that began to spread anti-Semitic propaganda, with preachers encouraging hatred of the Jews and blaming them for economic depression and any other problems in the country. (This was very similar to the way the Nazis in Germany used the Jews as scapegoats at a time when everyone was looking for someone or something to blame for the country's misfortunes.)

Reichantal went on to explain that as anti-Semitic propaganda started to spread throughout Slovakia, there were more and more attacks on Jews, even on the streets and in schools. As the number of violent attacks increased, they came to be seen as a 'normal' and unremarkable part of everyday life. More and more people came to accept the notion that the Jews really were the cause of all the problems, and accordingly ought to be despised, shunned and attacked. The more people who took this view, the easier it became for others to believe the same thing, until eventually the propaganda has completely displaced sense or reason, and ordinary people became mass murderers.

Social Proof and Uncertainty

Uncertainty and lack of clarity tends to intensify the 'wisdom of crowds' effect. When good information is scarce, you are even more inclined to believe whatever everyone else believes.

This 'uncertainty' effect is intensified if there is an emergency involved, with danger and injury to be taken into account. Your natural tendency is to look to others for clues about whether it really *is* an emergency and, if so, what's going on and the best response.

Incidentally, here's a little 'life tip' for you. In an emergency, the most effective course is to point to specific people and give them specific orders. Pointing to someone and saying 'You, call an ambulance!' is better than just saying, '*Someone* call an ambulance.'

Social Proof and Similarity

An interesting refinement of social proof is the idea of social similarity. We have seen that you tend to believe something if lots of other people seem to believe it. This tendency is even stronger if you *identify with* the other people concerned.

Suppose there are two groups, A and B. Group A believe that Gork chocolate makes you strong and fit, while Group B believe Gork chocolate is awful, and only popular with lonely, flabby social misfits. You will tend to follow the group you most closely identify with, *regardless of numbers*. If there are only a hundred people in your social group, and ten thousand in the other, you will still be biased towards the 'truth' as widely believed within your own group.

Psycholgists from Columbia University tested this using seemingly 'lost' wallets. They filled each wallet with enough details to find the owner, a bit of cash and a letter. The letter appeared to be from someone who had found the wallet to the owner, saying they were happy to return the wallet to him. Anyone who found the wallet and letter would think the finder had mislaid the wallet before being able to return it.

The letters stashed inside the wallets were not all the same. Some were written in standard American English, using expressions a typical native speaker might use. Others were written in broken English, and appeared to be from a foreigner who had recently moved to the country. The psychologists planted these wallets in various public places where they were likely to be found.

Seventy per cent of the wallets containing the 'American' letter were returned to the supposed owner, while only 33% of those containing the 'foreigner' letter were returned. This suggests that we are more likely to base our actions and behaviours on the actions of others when we perceive them to be similar to ourselves.

Positive And Negative Similarity

The notion that we all have this 'monkey see / monkey do' mentality may not be a comfortable one, but it doesn't always have to be seen in a negative light. In some cases, it can be put to good use. Psychologist Albert Bandura found that he could cure fear of dogs in children by showing them other children happily playing with dogs — either in real life or on video — with no negative consequences.

In one study, Bandura worked with a group of pre-school children who all had a severe fear of dogs. Every day, he showed them a twenty-minute video of a little boy playing with a dog. After only four days, about 70% of the children were willing to climb into a playpen containing a friendly dog. A month later, after the daily viewing of the video had stopped, the children were still very willing to play with the dog. Bandura found he could get even more successful results by showing videos of various children playing with their pet dogs (as opposed to just one). This is consistent with some of the other examples we have looked at — the greater the numbers involved, the stronger the effect of social proof seems to be.

Contaminated Proof

Ideas can contaminate one another. We have seen that you are more prone to believe something if you think lots of other people believe it. But if you become aware of some contrary views and rival notions, you may begin to doubt whether you're seeing the whole picture. For this reason, the persuader or propaganda expert doesn't just seek to make sure lots of people believe Concept X, but also strives to extinguish rival concepts — or at least keep them some distance away.

This is why cult leaders often isolate their members, both by living in remote places and by encouraging members to cut all ties with outsiders. If you only ever meet people who support a given idea, and never meet anyone who dissents or offers an alternative idea, you are more likely to believe it and trust it.

Imaginary Proof

It is interesting to note that this tendency to trust the views of others, and to rely on the judgement of crowds, works perfectly well whether the crowd is real or entirely made up. In other words, you are prone to going along with the flow of the crowd even when it doesn't really exist.

Robert Cialdini demonstrated this experimentally in 2007. He created five different cards to be left in hotel rooms asking guests to reuse their towels, even if only once during their stay. The five cards offered different reasons to reuse towels:

- Help the hotel save energy.

- Help save the environment.

- Partner with us to help save the environment.

- Help save resources for future generations.

- Join your fellow guests in helping save the environment. (In a study conducted in fall 2003, 75% of guests participated in our resource savings programme by using their towel more than once).

Of the hotel guests who received the first card, emphasising the benefit *to the hotel*, only 16% reused their towels.

Of the hotel guest who received the fifth card, 44% reused their towels. When the wording on the fifth card was slightly adjusted to say 75% of the guests *who stayed in that particular room* participated in the scheme, the success rate increased to 49%.

Even though each guest read the card individually, and was not placed under any pressure from any other hotel guest to participate, the effect of social pressure remained.

Pluralistic Ignorance

The tendency to rely on what everyone else thinks, or what everyone else is doing, leads to the intriguing concept of 'pluralistic ignorance'.

Our sense of social responsibility helps us make good choices — or at least it does *some* of the time. Unfortunately, when we are in a position of *shared* responsibility we may fail to act the way we ought to. This was vividly demonstrated in an experiment conducted by Richard Nisbett.

His experiment involved groups of six volunteers, one of whom was an actor. Each of the six volunteers sat in their own individual booth. The first person was given two minutes to talk about their life and problems, after which their microphone was switched off and the next person's microphone was switched on for their two-minute monologue. Everyone could hear everyone else's talk.

Following a script prepared by Nesbitt, the actor spoke first — detailing his life's struggles and admitting, to his embarrassment, that he suffered from stress-induced seizures that put his life at risk. Once all the other volunteers had had their two minutes, the actor had his chance to speak again. He said he was feeling very tense and then proceeded to fake a seizure, begging for someone to help him. He made choking sounds as if he were in serious difficulties, at which time his microphone switched off and the next person's microphone switched on as usual.

There were fifteen participants in the experiment (aside from the actor). Only four of them responded immediately and tried to get help. Five of the fifteen only emerged from their booths well after the volunteer would have already died and six of them never moved from their booths at all.

It would be easy to write off the eleven volunteers who didn't make any effort to help as terrible people, but this wouldn't be fair. What the experiment showed is that when others hear the same call for help as we do, we feel relieved of our responsibility to take action.

Social Proof and Cold Reading

Social proof and the wisdom of crowds also assist the cold reading industry. Many psychics take care to establish that they have been in business a long time and have given lots and lots of readings, and that they have a number of VIP and celebrity clients. The message is loud and clear: 'lots of people believe in my powers, therefore you should too'.

In some cases, these claims of impressive popularity and a long list of celebrity clients may well be true. In other cases, the facts might be very slightly embellished for PR purposes. When I say, 'very slightly embellished for PR purposes', I mean 'totally made up, and having about as much to do with reality as flying pink unicorns'.

What can be said with certainty is that no psychic in the history of the psychic industry has ever passed up the opportunity to be photographed alongside a celebrity or so-called VIP client. There is a phrase that has never been uttered in the history of cold reading, and here it is: 'Yes, I suppose a photo with a famous person like yourself would be terribly good for publicity and help to bolster my credibility... but you know what? Let's put the camera away and just keep this between ourselves.'

There is, of course, no logic to celebrity endorsements. Most are purely commercial arrangements (hence insincere), and the rest tend to suffer from grievous lack of relevant expertise. The fact that a popular comedian's face appears in an advert for car insurance tells you nothing, unless the comedian spends his spare time studying the insurance market in some detail and impartially comparing the merits of different policies.

When it comes to the psychic readings industry, the nonsensicality of the celebrity endorsement becomes even more glaringly obvious. The fact that someone stars in a popular soap opera does not, in and of itself, qualify them to pronounce upon the authenticity of psychic gifts, or to overturn a hundred years or so of scientific research.

Authority

So far we've seen that if you want to get people to comply with your ideas or directions, it's a good idea to exploit the 'social proof' phenomenon and convey the idea that lots of people, especially lots of people *just like you*, are already on board.

Another good idea is to use authority. You have a tendency to obey authority figures for two fairly obvious reasons. The first is that at one point in your life, when you were very young, small and helpless, you relied on 'authority figures' to survive. Your parents were the ones feeding you, giving you shelter and fighting off the wolves (figuratively speaking, unless you had an exceptionally unusual upbringing).

The second is that from a very early age you have probably been taught and conditioned to obey a range of authority figures: parents, older siblings and family members, teachers, religious leaders, the police and even people such as newsreaders and political leaders. You have also been trained to respect authority props and symbols: 'Stop' signs, 'No entry' signs, hazard tape, 'Keep off the grass' notices and so on.

Milgram Experiment

This strongly imprinted respect for authority can work to your advantage, of course. It can even mean the difference between life and death. Unfortunately, it can also be abused.

This was famously demonstrated in an experiment conducted by Stanley Milgram in 1961. He arranged for participants to take part in a teaching exercise involving pairs of words. The participants were in separate rooms and could not see one another, but were able to hear one another via microphones and speakers. When the 'learner' made a mistake in the word test, the 'teacher' was instructed by an authority figure in a white lab coat to press a button which he was told gave the 'learner' an electric shock. In reality, the 'learner' was just an actor pretending to receive the electric shocks. Even when the 'learner' pretended to be in great pain, or even claimed to have a heart condition, many participants continued to administer the electric shocks when directed to do so. They obeyed the authority figure, even though they were apparently causing great pain and suffering.

Outdated Authority

Another problem with respect for authority is that you may fail to update it or recognise its limits. It is perfectly possible to retain a respect for a specific source of authority long after it has ceased to be relevant.

Not too long ago, there was a significant campaign aimed at fighting animal abuse in circuses. Videos circulated on the Internet of trainers being cruel to the animals supposedly in their care. In a small number of instances the animals made an effort to retaliate, but in the majority of cases the animals displayed signs of 'learnt hopelessness' and simply took the abuse heaped upon them.

The owners of elephants use this principle to ensure that the adult elephants in their care do not use their great strength to break free. From birth, each baby elephant is chained to a small stake in the ground. As much as it may try to break free, the baby elephant soon learns that the chain is just too strong. It learns that it cannot escape when it is chained to a stake in the ground.

When the elephant has grown to be an adult, it is far bigger and stronger. However, even when chained to something quite small, it does not attempt to escape because it 'knows' that it cannot do so — and in fact has known this from birth.

To some extent, we are not much smarter than the adult elephants that fail to realise they could easily escape from their constraints. We retain a childlike instinct to automatically obey authority, and our System 1 thinking allows the chains of obedience to hold us down.

Fake Authority

Advertisers frequently exploit both our acquired respect for authority and our inability to reserve this respect for appropriate contexts. For example, doctors enjoy high status in our society. Hence someone with a product to advertise may hire an actor who looks like a genial, reassuring but authoritative doctor to say why Gork Headache Tablets are the best. When you see the advert, on one level you know he's just an actor who has been given a white coat and told to read some lines. On another level, your System 1 thinking kicks into action and says, 'Doctor > good source of info re health > buy this product.'

You may think you're far too smart to be seduced by such transparent tricks. However, the only reason such ruses are still used is that sufficient numbers of people are easily taken in by them. If they didn't work, these kinds of ads would have died out long ago.

If you wonder why these kinds of ads still work so well, even though we all know about the fakery involved, the answer has a lot to do with the idea of *automatic obedience*. When you were growing up, you didn't just experience a range of bossy authority figures — you also learned that obedience was *mostly* in your best interests and *mostly* led to good rewards. You may have had some complaints here and there about always being told what to do, but you also figured out that all the rules kept you safe, kept you out of trouble, meant more rewards and fewer punishments and won you lots of praise for being so good.

After a while, you didn't need to keep doing the calculation anymore: you understood that going along with authority was a pretty good idea, and rebelling against it was a fairly bad / dangerous / painful one. This was a good development, in that you stopped wasting time figuring out something that didn't need to be figured out again. It was also a bad one, in that you adopted some patterns of behaviour that other people can and do exploit. They can trigger your System 1 thinking and play on your automatic respect for authority. The result? Actors pretending to be doctors and telling you that Gork Headache Tablets work best.

You are just as vulnerable to the signs and symbols of authority as to the various personifications of it. You don't just respond to the person hired to play the role of a doctor. You also respond to his crisply starched white coat, the stethoscope loitering pointlessly around his neck, the clean clinical environment without a speck of dirt in sight, the clipboard and the authoritative tone of voice. All these elements convey 'authority'.

Incidentally, having mentioned actors pretending to be doctors, it is worth remembering that even genuine authority figures can be hopelessly misled and misleading, especially when powerful interests have money to spend. It is not so very long since real doctors, with proper qualifications, were popping up in press adverts for cigarettes.

Responses to Authority

Our response to authority often works in interesting ways. A British university once put an 'honesty box' in the office canteen, together with a list of prices for tea and coffee. Anyone who helped themselves to a drink was asked to pay for it by putting the correct money in the box. A banner was placed over the price list, featuring a different picture each week. Sometimes it was a picture of flowers, while at other times it was a picture of a watchful pair of eyes. When the 'Eyes' banner was in place, the people using the canteen put almost three times as much money in box as they did when the 'Flowers' banner was in place.

The picture of eyes primed those involved to feel social pressure (social proof), or to be more obedient (authority).

Authority Props

I said before that you respond not just to authority, but to the signs, symbols and representations of authority. It is surprising just how many different forms these can take.

Height

People often regard tall people as having natural authority. This could be because when you were young all the authority figures in your life were bigger than you, so you learned to associate size with authority.

This association between height and authority leads to many forms of fakery. Some men wear 'lifts' in their shoes to appear taller than they really are. Some women seek shoes with very high heels for the same reason. In offices throughout the land, people try to gain and express power by using a higher chair, a bigger desk or a larger room. The equation is always the same: bigger means more authoritative.

Language

Research in the field of linguistics has shown that authority figures tend to have a greater vocabulary than other people. There is certainly a common perception that a well-spoken person has an authoritative advantage. This leads to some attempts at fakery, such as people peppering their speech with long words and fancy expressions in the hope that they will seem more important. This is of course a sophistic and nugatory postulation.

There is an interesting parallel here with non-verbal communication. Research into body language suggests there is a correlation between a person's command of the spoken word and the number of gestures they use to communicate their message. The high status individual is able to articulate her meaning very clearly and therefore requires fewer gestures; the low status individual lacks the same expressive vocabulary, and tries to compensate by using more gestures.

Clothes and Accessories

The clothes you wear can convey a great deal about your status, or the status you *think* you have. We can't help being affected by clothing, uniforms and anything else that suggests 'high status'.

In an experiment conducted in Texas, a man purposefully broke the law by crossing the road against the traffic signal. He wanted to see how many other people would follow his example and cross at the same time (thereby technically breaking the law). Sometimes the man wore a 'low status' outfit of simple slacks and a casual shirt, while on other occasions he wore a 'high status' smart business suit and tie. When he was smartly dressed, three and a half times as many people followed his example as when he was wearing the 'low status' outfit.

Titles

Titles are simultaneously the most difficult and the easiest symbols of authority to acquire. They are difficult to acquire legitimately, via many years of study, but very easy to acquire illegitimately. Plenty of people have 'awarded' themselves titles purely to convey an image of authority, high status or deep knowledge.

In South Africa, traditional names often relate to an aspect of the child's birth. For example, if the parents struggled to conceive a child, they might name their baby Sibusiso ('blessing'). I once worked with a man whose first name was literally 'Doctor' — perhaps because of the involvement a doctor had in his birth. He was a fairly poor gentleman and his attire showed it. I was always amused whenever I introduced people to him. I could see that at first they tended to stereotype him, based on his somewhat humble appearance. As soon as I said, 'By the way, his name is Doctor —', their attitude changed immediately! The very sound of the title 'Doctor' was enough to radically transform how they perceived his status.

The Halo Effect

Any discussion of authority, and how we respond to it, has to include a fascinating phenomenon known as the halo effect. This is a common type of bias in which approval of one trait or aspect of a person leads to the approval of other, entirely separate traits — including ones that you may not have seen or know much about. For example, if you like the look of a politician and the way he talks, you are likely to approve of his politics (even if you don't know much about them) and to assume he is of good character or someone you can relate to (even if in fact he is nothing like you, lives an entirely different life and wouldn't give you so much as the time of day).

A very common manifestation of the halo effect is that we feel drawn to confident people and tend to assume positive things about them. When you meet someone who exudes great personal confidence, you tend to feel they are trustworthy and credible. This happens despite the fact that confidence, like other virtues, can be faked.

Authority in Mentalism

The subject of authority is close to my heart, and the same goes for all my brothers and sisters in the world of magical and mind-reading entertainment. Let me explain why.

When I'm on stage, I have to maintain a sense of authority to do the things that I do. One reason is that I am constantly telling people to do things: think of a number, choose one of these pictures, focus on a childhood memory and so on. I have to orchestrate all these actions in a certain way or else the show won't be very entertaining. Also, reading minds and anticipating people's choices involves many different psychological strategies, but one of them is that I have to exercise a degree of control over the people who take part in my demonstrations. There are two ways to do this. One is to do it fairly obviously, and come across as a rather cold, dislikeable control freak. The other is to do it in rather subtle ways, so that nobody minds or notices. I try very hard to do it the second way.

Likeability

On many websites and online forums, you can click a 'Like' button to show that you approve of what someone else has posted. We all love to received these 'Likes' — the more we receive the more influence we feel we have. As it turns out, 'liking' is just as powerful a weapon of influence in the real world as it is in the digital world.

I got my first taste of this principle when I was just out of school and got involved with a network marketing organisation. My mentors used to say, 'People like to do business with people they know, like and trust.' I have since heard this said at many sales and success seminars.

My marketing team and I often arranged to meet at the home of a sales prospect or someone we were hoping to recruit. These 'home meetings' were a very good idea because the prospect usually invited friends and family to the meeting. Hence, they were surrounded by people they liked and these feelings of safe, easy familiarity got transferred to me and my team. As a result, we tended to be very successful at recruiting people and selling our products.

The Shaklee Corporation is a network marketing organisation for health and nutrition products (though not one with which I have ever had any association). Their sales manual says:

> *"Phoning or calling on a prospect and being able to say that 'So-and-so, a friend of his, felt he would benefit by giving you a few moments of his time' is virtually as good as a sale 50% made before you enter."*

In brief, familiar faces, and introductions from familiar faces, can help us to sell and persuade. But if you don't have that personal introduction, how can you get people to like you?

Likeable Looks

Not surprisingly, looks count for a lot. We automatically assume good-looking people have favourable traits such as talent, kindness, honesty and intelligence. We also tend to think that 'good looks' equals 'a good person', which is scary and incorrect.

Because we like attractive people, and tend to comply more readily with people we like, sales training courses usually include grooming tips and techniques, and image consultants enjoy a thriving trade.

Liked by Association

Another way to get people to like you is to give them good news. This is one of those quirks of human interaction that shouldn't work, and isn't fair, but it does. If you give someone good news that cheers them up, you tend to be become associated with those happy feelings. Conversely, if you give someone bad news they will dislike you, even though you are just the messenger.

Cold readers are well aware of this principle of association. However, skilled readers don't just ensure their reading is an endless litany of good news and bright forecasts. That would lack credibility, even by the rather lax standards of the psychic industry. Everyone knows that life isn't all roses and rainbows, all the time. Therefore the artful reader makes sure the reading features *some* very *gentle* traces of *mild* concern about possible adversity, while ensuring that the overall picture is very positive, bright, happy and optimistic.

Positive and Negative

The principle of association applies equally to both positive and negative types of association. If someone becomes associated with either good or bad news, even if this happens through no will of their own, their popularity and reputation can go up or down accordingly.

One common example is the fawning adulation that tends to accrue to an actor lucky enough to get cast in a popular TV show. In truth, that particular actor might have very little to do with the fact that the show is a hit. He had nothing to do with devising the series or inventing the characters. He doesn't write the script, and has nothing to do with the production, direction, sets, costumes or props. Reduced to its basics, his role is to wear what someone tells him to wear, stand where someone tells him to stand, and then say what someone told him to say. Nonetheless, he may well find himself achieving exalted celebrity status and the subject of hero worship.

Needless to add, the notion of glory-by-association takes us into very subjective and judgemental areas. In my own case, if I meet someone and happen to discover that they play chess, I tend to warm to that person automatically even though I haven't played chess seriously for more than ten years.

People also associate *similarity* with *liking* someone. In other words, if I think you're quite similar to me in various significant ways, I'll be inclined to like you. All things being equal, people are partisan and tribal. They prefer their own sex, their own culture, their own locality and their own everything. To be sufficiently similar to come across as 'one of us' is to win popularity in a very easy way.

This raises an interesting question: how *much* similarity is sufficient to elicit a sympathetic or positive opinion? To test this, Robert Cialdini and John Finch conducted an experiment on some students. They worked with each student individually. They gave him or her a summary of the life of the infamous Grigori Rasputin, aka The Mad Monk of Russia, including all his evil deeds and terrible escapades. The student was then asked to rate Rasputin's character. Cialdini and Finch gave all the students exactly the same information about this striking character from the days of Tsarist Russia. However, they told half the students that they *shared the same birthday* as Rasputin. Those who were under the impression they shared the Mad Monk's birthday gave him a much more positive character assessment than the others.

It is surprising to think that such a relatively trivial kind of 'similarity' as having the same birthday can influence our perception and judgement, but it can and it does. This is why many politicians, marketing experts and even conmen aim to make you believe they have something in common with you.

For the ambitious persuader, the lesson is obvious: try to make someone think you are like them, and they will be more likely to like you, to trust you and to buy from you.

Reciprocation

In social psychology, reciprocation refers to our sense that we ought to match one positive action with another, equivalent positive action. If someone does something nice for you, you feel you ought to respond in kind. In lieu of any other factors, someone striking up a conversation with you is a nice, friendly thing to do, so you feel that you ought to respond, even if you'd really prefer not to.

Noted archaeologist Richard Leakey ascribes the essence of what makes us human to the reciprocal system:

> "We are human because our ancestors learned to share their food and their skills in an honoured network of obligation."

Cultural anthropologists Lionel Tiger and Robin Fox refer to this 'web of indebtedness' as 'a uniquely human adaptive mechanism'. They point out that, among other things, 'it allows for the division of labour, the exchange of diverse forms of goods, the exchange of different services (making it possible for experts to develop) and the creation of clusters of interdependencies that bind individuals together into effective units'.

This same principle of shared, mutual indebtedness makes it possible for sophisticated and coordinated systems of aid to develop, as well as defence pacts and trade agreements. These social developments clearly bring immense benefits for all concerned. It's therefore not surprising that we all feel a sense of reciprocation is a fundamental part of our civilised nature. A corollary to this is that we penalise those who appear to break the 'rules' of reciprocation.

- We use disparaging terms such as moocher, freeloader, sponge, parasite, slacker and loafer.

- There is great social stigma attached to being labelled as someone who takes and makes no effort to give anything back.

The rule of reciprocity can work in strange ways. For example, even if someone gives you something you didn't ask for (and maybe didn't even want), you still feel obliged to repay the 'kindness' or the 'favour' involved.

166

Restaurant Reciprocation

This was demonstrated in an experiment conducted by David Strohmetz of Monmouth University. He divided restaurant goers into groups defined by the number of after-dinner sweets or candies they received with their bill. One group received one sweet from the waiter. The second group received two. The third group received one sweet, then the waiter returned to give them another sweet, 'Just for you'.

The number of sweets the customers received affected how generous their tips were. Compared with customers who received no sweets, those who received just one sweet tipped around 3% more. Those in the second group left tips about 14% higher. However, those in the third group tipped on average 23% higher. The simple act of giving away an extra sweet, but making it seem like it was a spontaneous 'special treat', made all the difference.

Obligation to Receive

The essence of the reciprocation rule is that we feel obliged to repay: you give me something, I ought to give you something back. However, when it comes to persuasion games, the most significant factor is not the felt obligation to *repay* so much as the obligation to *receive*. If someone offers you something, you feel obliged to take it. There are many examples of this:

- companies that send uninvited gifts;

- charities that send out personalised address labels, calendars, pens, greeting cards, key rings... and then ask for a donation in return; and

- businesses that send clients and prospects bottles of wine, free holidays and invitations to prestigious events.

There is strong cultural pressure to accept a gift, even an unwanted one. Note that this places all the control in the hands of the giver, not the receiver. The giver can trigger the reciprocation response at any time, just by giving something to you.

This technique has many guises. Consider the 'free sample' marketing technique. A small sample of a product is given away free, ostensibly so the customer can see if he likes it. However, the free sample constitutes a gift, and therefore tends to trigger the reciprocation instinct.

Give to Receive

I was once visiting a museum in Ho Chi Minh (Saigon) City. I walked past an elderly Asian lady who offered me a flower with its petals folded to create a beautiful design. Captivated by her smile and charm, I was about to take the flower when I suddenly realised what was going on. I looked down and sure enough the woman had a piece of paper bearing a message in English asking for money. Instead of taking the flower, I leaned forward, inhaled its fragrance and walked away.

I quietly observed this flower lady for some time. She managed to get just about everyone to take a flower from her, at which point she asked for money. Everyone who took a flower had to make a donation. If they tried to give it back, the lady refused and insisted it was a gift — thereby triggering the reciprocation instinct. Many people, not wishing to get into a protracted argument over a flower, handed over some money just to get away.

This strategy, which we can refer to as 'give to receive', can trigger unfair exchanges. The small initial favour or offering can lead to a sense of obligation to offer a much larger favour in return.

A Cornell University study by Professor Dennis Regan examined this phenomenon in detail. Regan set up a mock experiment on art appreciation involving two participants — one of which was actually his associate Joe. During a break in the mock experiment, Joe bought himself and the other participant a soft drink, saying, 'I asked the experimenter if I could get myself a cola and he said it was okay, so I got one for you, too.' Later, Joe asked the other participant if he would be willing to buy some raffle tickets as he was trying to win a prize for selling the most tickets.

This exact scenario was repeated with another set of participants, the only difference being that Joe did *not* buy the other participant a drink. He did still try to sell the raffle tickets. The volunteers for whom Joe bought a soft drink bought twice as many raffle tickets, and in many cases the value of the tickets they bought was greater than the cost of the soft drink Joe had bought for them.

Clearly, most people dislike being indebted or obliged to anyone else. We feel a strong sense of wanting to 'clear the debt' and 'settle the score'. In fact, this can be so intense that we may be willing to give back more than we received, purely to remove the emotional burden of debt.

Reject and Retreat

Another variation of the reciprocation game is the 'reject / retreat' technique. I want you to agree to a particular request. I start by making a much larger request that I am fairly sure you will turn down. After you have refused the deal, I submit a much smaller request that is, in reality, the one I wanted you to accept all along. One positive aspect of this technique is that you will tend to feel that you determined the final agreement (by rejecting my first request). For this reason, you will be more likely to honour the final agreement we reached.

If you want to use this strategy, you have to be careful. Research at Bar-Ilan University, Israel, showed that if the initial demands are so extreme as to be considered unreasonable, the strategy fails. The 'unreasonable' party is seen as lacking good faith, and any subsequent retreat from the 'unreasonable' position seems contrived and lacking in integrity, and is therefore not reciprocated.

The truly skilled negotiator makes an initial offer that seems reasonable but is still sufficiently exaggerated to allow for a series of reciprocal concessions that will lead to a final deal both parties can readily accept.

Reciprocation and Cold Reading

Some people suppose that during a 'psychic' reading, the cold reader does almost all of the talking while the client sits there listening. One side gives, the other takes, and everyone's happy. In reality, few readings, if any, follow this pattern. The far more typical pattern is this:

- the psychic makes a statement of some kind, and waits for feedback or prompts for it;

- the client offers feedback, both verbal and non-verbal; and

- the psychic shapes her reading accordingly, and can either discuss her last statement or move on to the next one.

Most clients never realise how much information and feedback they provide during the reading. In one of his demonstrations for a television documentary, author Ian Rowland was asked to pose as a psychic and give readings to two different women. The readings were videotaped. When the two women were subsequently interviewed, they both gave sincere assurances that they had been careful not to respond to questions or provide much feedback. In fact, the video playback showed that they had been providing more or less *constant* feedback from start to finish, as well as supplying a lot of personal information. The women were sincere in their assurances, and not trying to mislead anyone. They just happened to be mistaken about what had really happened during the reading. This is commonplace in the psychic industry.

Psychics love getting feedback from their clients. It helps them to decide which themes the client clearly wants them to focus on, and what sort of answers or reassurances they are looking for.

Cultivating Feedback

Given that psychics like feedback and plenty of it, they don't just passively hope that the client will be so kind as to provide it. Instead, they make it their business to cultivate as much feedback as possible. There are various ways to do this, but by far the most common and productive is to include plenty of feedback prompts. These take various forms, from asking a direct question to using what Ian Rowland refers to as a veiled question: phrasing something so it *sounds* like a statement when in fact it's simply another request for information.

These various prompts for feedback work because we are social, gregarious animals and need to communicate successfully with the rest of our 'tribe' to survive. Hence, we feel a sense of obligation to respond to verbal communication. Even if a complete stranger comes up to you and tries to chat, you feel at least faintly obliged to respond — albeit as briefly as possible before trying to walk away and avoid further interaction.

Commitment

If I can get you to make a commitment to something, even in quite a minor way, you will then tend to behave in a way that is consistent with that commitment, no matter what. In addition, the more public the initial commitment is, the greater the perceived need to be consistent, for fear of being considered fickle, weak or inconsistent. This sort of stubbornness can arise even in situations where accuracy should be more important than consistency.

The more effort you put into a commitment, the more strongly it will influence your attitude and behaviour. If I get you to write out your commitment, this requires more effort so you will feel a greater tendency to stick to it.

An interesting illustration of this point arose when South Africa introduced a new Consumer Protection Act (CPA), which enabled consumers to return unused goods for any reason at all within seven days of purchase. Retailers didn't like this because they were suddenly inundated with people returning goods they had simply decided they didn't really want after all. What the retailers wanted was a way to discourage customers from bringing things back even though the new law said they could.

They found a good way to do this was to get the *customer* to fill out the sales form or contract instead of the salesman. This led to a significant reduction in the number of returns and cancelled contracts. Because the customers had made more effort to buy the goods, which corresponds to making more of a commitment, they were psychologically far less inclined to reverse their decision.

Once we have made a choice or taken a stand, we will encounter personal and interpersonal pressures to behave consistently with that commitment. Those pressures will cause us to respond in ways that justify our earlier decision.

Foot in the Door

In 1966, the *Journal of Personality and Social Psychology* published a study by Jonathan Freedman and Scott Fraser that illustrated the power of what has become known as the 'foot in the door' technique.

This technique involves preceding your large requests with small, easy requests to create an attitude of compliance before asking for what you *really* want.

To demonstrate this, Freedman and Fraser had an experimenter pose as a volunteer worker going door to door in a neighbourhood asking homeowners to let them to place a large billboard on their lawns saying 'Drive Carefully'. Unsurprisingly, more than 80% of the residents refused.

However, in a different neighbourhood they managed to get a 76% success rate by using the more subtle 'foot in the door' approach. First, they asked each homeowner if they could put up a small sign on their lawn saying, 'Be a Safe Driver'. It was such a small thing to ask that nearly all of them agreed. Two weeks later, when they were asked about the giant billboard, even when faced with an 'example' of the billboard which was purposefully designed to obscure most of the house and was badly written, the overwhelming majority agreed to it.

There's more to the story. Freedman and Fraser tried another neighbourhood and this time the first request to each home owner was just to sign a petition to keep California beautiful. The vast majority agreed to sign. Later on, when they were asked for permission to put up the billboard, 50% agreed to the really terrible sign being placed on their lawn. Even though the first request (sign this petition) had *nothing* to do with the second one (let us put this hideous billboard on your lawn), it was enough to affect the feelings of the homeowners. Signing the petition made them feel like good citizens, who would take action to improve their neighbourhood. When presented with the billboard request, they wanted to remain consistent to this idea of who they were, and so they complied.

Gilan's Persuasion Tips

Here are three simple tips for you based on this chapter:

- Remember the five keys to compliance: social proof, authority, likeability, reciprocation and commitment. They all have a part to play in your persuasive campaigns.

- Of the five strategies in this chapter, social proof is perhaps the most important of all. It can radically transform any persuasive strategy. You don't have to persuade the customer to buy the car; you just have to convince him that many *other* people, just like him, have bought the car or want to.

- Try to be likeable. As well as being a very good persuasive strategy, this is also just good life advice. Don't be misled by the fact that one or two unpleasant people manage to be successful. The vast majority of successful people understand the importance of being nice, helpful, pleasant, kind and respectful.

Summary

In this chapter we looked at five ways to get other people to comply with your wishes.

We explored social proof and the wisdom of crowds — the fact that persuasion can be contagious, and that people will be happy to trust you so long as they know many other people also trust you.

We also looked at authority, likeability, reciprocation and commitment, and how these factors might apply to various situations.

You can never get all the people to comply with your wishes, all the time —and in any case only a crazed dictator would want this kind of power. But by using the techniques in this chapter wisely and judiciously, you may be able to win compliance on one or two occasions when you really need it.

12: The Gork Approach

"Example is not the main thing in influencing others. It is the only thing."

— *Albert Schweitzer*

What's My Name?

We have covered a lot of ground in this book. I can't summarise all of the persuasion techniques, tips and strategies in this book in one short, simple system. What I *can* do is share with you a drastically simplified approach to persuasion, and to people, that I devised some time ago. It doesn't suit all situations, but then again no system ever does.

You can use this approach as a way to remember a few key principles that will help you to be more persuasive. You can also use it to see if your current influence and persuasion strategies can perhaps be improved in any way.

Not surprisingly, I call it the Gork Approach.

G: Give shortcuts

People constantly seek shortcuts to help them process the vast amounts of data in the world around them. Use influence and persuasion strategies that engage primarily with people's System 1 thinking, and allow *their* heuristics to work in *your* favour.

Keep in mind the various common shortcuts that people enjoy taking, such as:

- Confirmation bias — they select the evidence that fits what they already believe, or want to be true.

- Cognitive ease — the easier it is to understand and believe something, the more likely people are to believe it. Clarity, repetition and even rhyming assist cognitive ease.

- Comparison — people judge the value of something *relative* to something else. If you show someone two items for sale, show them the expensive one first. If you want someone to choose between two options, add a third 'decoy' option that is less attractive than the one you want them to choose.

- Scarcity — if people believe something is rare or soon to be unavailable, they want it more. This applies to physical items, opportunities and even to people.

O: Offer scope and potential for meaning

People constantly try to find patterns and meaning in the world, and can even find meaning where there is little or none (castles in clouds). Learn from the masters of cold reading and present information to people so that they can create significant meaning for themselves. This is especially powerful if you also create the right shortcuts in their mind so that they connect the dots that *you* want them to connect.

R: Redefine perception and expectation

A person's expectation and perception becomes their reality.

Remember to reframe the conversation so that the other person can align with your position. Framing is just one of many good techniques mentioned in this book, but it's one of the most versatile and fun to play with. Every conversation you have, with any person or prospect, has a frame of some sort around it. Make sure that frame is helping you to achieve your persuasion goals.

Use the halo effect to realign a person's expectations about you and your abilities, based on the fact that everyone transfers credibility from one area of your life to another completely unrelated area.

Also, use priming and anchoring to write certain thoughts or emotions into someone's mind.

K: get Kreative

I know that 'creative' doesn't normally start with a 'k'. I just felt like spelling it in a kreative way.

To be a good persuader, you often need to think quickly on your feet, and use the principles in this book in a creative way. The good news is that the more you practise these techniques, the more creative you will become. You will start to apply good persuasive strategies at an intuitive level, without thinking about it. You will notice that you become a more persuasive, more successful person in every area of your life.

That's it. That's the GORK approach to influence and persuasion. It's short, it's neat and it works like a treat. Good luck!

Suggested Reading

Dan Ariely, *Predictably Irrational*

Susan Blackmore, *Adventures of a Parapsychologist*

Christopher Chabris and Daniel Simons, *The Invisible Gorilla*

Robert Cialdini, *Influence*

Kevin Dutton, *Flipnosis*

Nicholas Humphrey, *The Inner Eye*

Daniel Kahneman, *Thinking, Fast and Slow*

Lamar Keene, *The Psychic Mafia*

John Maxwell, *The 21 Irrefutable Laws of Leadership*

John Maxwell, *Becoming a Person of Influence*

Ian Rowland, *The Full Facts Book of Cold Reading*

Richard Wiseman, *Paranormality*

References

Herring gull
Tinbergen, Nikolaas, and Perdeck, Albert C, 'On the Stimulus Situation Releasing the Begging Response in the Newly Hatched Herring Gull Chick (Larus a. argentatus Pont.).' *Behavior*, 3, pp 1-38. 1950.

Photocopy queue experiment
A more systematic treatment of Langer's Xerox study and her conceptualisation of it can be found in Langer (1989).

Thatcher illusion
Thompson, P. 'Margaret Thatcher: A New Illusion'. *Perception*. 1980.

Sex sells
McCleneghan, J Sean. 'Selling Sex to College Females: Their Attitudes about Cosmopolitan and Glamour'. *The Social Science Journals*, 40(2), pp 317-325. 2003.

Basketball players and bankers
Beyth-Marom, Ruth, and Dekel, Shlomith, *An Elementary Approach to Thinking under Certainty*. Hillsdale, NJ: Erlbaum, 1985.

Heuristics
More information on cognitive shortcuts can been found by reading
Daniel Kahneman and Amos Tversky's 'On the Psychology of
Prediction.' *Psychological Review*, 80, pp 237-251. 1973.

Systems 1 and 2 thinking
Stanovich, Keith E, and West, Richard F. 'Individual Differences in
Reasoning: Implications for the Rationality Debate'. *Behavioural and
Brain Sciences*, 23, pp 645-665. 2000.

Debunking "draw a picture"
Chapman, LJ, and Chapman, JP. 'Genesis of Popular but Erroneous
Psychodiagnostic Observations'. *Journal of Abnormal Psychology*, 72,
pp 193-204. 1967.

Availability heuristics
Schwarz, N, Bless, H, Strack, F, Klumpp, G, Rittenauer-Schatka, H, and
Simons, A. 'Ease of Retrieval as Information: Another Look at the
Availability Heuristic'. *Journal of Personality and Social Psychology*, 61,
pp 195–202. 1991.

Mood effect on judgement
Schwarz, N, and Clore, GL. 'Mood, Misattribution and Judgement of
Well-being: Informative and Directive Functions of Affective States'.
Journal of Personality and Social Psychology, 45, pp 513–523. 1983.

Cognitive ease
Reber, R, and Schwarz, N. 'Effects of Perceptual Fluency on Judgements
of Truth'. *Consciousness and Cognition: An International Journal*, 8, pp
338–342. 1999.

Egocentric bias
Myers, DG. *Social Psychology*. New York: McGraw-Hill Higher
Education, 2008.

Remote associates test (RAT)
Mednick, Sarnoff. 'The Associative Basis of Creativity'. *Psychological
Review*, 69(3), pp 220–232. 1962.

Suggestion (mint experiment)
Slosson, EE. 'A Lecture Experiment in Hallucinations'. *Psychology
Review*, 6, pages 407-408. 1899.

Placebo (wine price experiment)
Plassman, Hilke, O'Doherty, John P, Shiv, Baba, and Rangel, Antonio.
'Marketing Actions Can Modulate Neural Representations of
Experienced Pleasantness'. *Proceedings of the National Academy of
Sciences of the United States of America*, 105(3), pp 1,050-1,054. 2008

Pavlov's dog
Pavlov, IP. *Conditional Reflexes*. New York: Dover Publications, 1927 and 1960.

Line experiment
Asch, Solomon E, 'Opinions and Social Pressure'. *Scientific American*, 193, pp 31-35. 1955.

Dog phobia treatment
Bandura, Grusec and Menlove (1967) and Bandura and Menlove (1968) for full descriptions.

Pluralistic ignorance: helping experiment
Nisbett, R, and Wilson. T. 'Telling More Than We Can Know: Verbal Reports on Mental Processes'. *Psychological Review*, 84(3), pp 231-259. 1977.

Milgram's experiment
All variations of Milgram's experiment, from the basic one to several others, can be found in Milgram's book, *Obedience to Authority*, 1974. Subsequent research has been done on obedience, which can be found in Blass (1991).

Authority, clothes and accessories
The experiment conducted with the man crossing the street illegally was conducted by Lefkowitz, Blake and Mouton (1955).

The order in which you give information
Lemann, Nicholas. 'The Word Lab'. *The New Yorker*, Oct 16 2000.

Tips at restaurants
Strohmetz, David B, Rind, Bruce, Fisher, Reed, and Lynn, Michael. 'Sweetening the Till: The Use of Candy to Increase Restaurant Tipping'. *Journal of Applied Social Psychology*, 32, pp 300-309. 2002.

Reciprocation, Coke and raffle experiment
The experiment is reported formally in Regan (1971).

Meaningless lecture
Naftulin, DH, Ware, JE, and Donnelly, FA. 'The Doctor Fox Lecture: A Paradigm of Educational Seduction'. *Journal of Medical Education*, 48, pp 630-635. 1973.

Commitment and the 'Drive Safely' billboard experiment
Freedman and Fraser published their data in the *Journal of Personality and Social Psychology* in 1966.

Thanks and Acknowledgements

There are many people who have directly or indirectly contributed to this book and served as great sources of influence and inspiration in my life, whether they are aware of it or not. I would love to mention them all but that would require a book by itself.

First of all, I want to thank my family, who continue to be the biggest influences in my life: my parents, Monty and Avrille; my siblings, Liora, Ari and Dana, and their spouses, Shaun, Nicki and Zev. I must also thank my extended family who live all around the world and keep in touch with me so often: Jee, Ivan, Jordi and Dayne. Special mention goes to my beloved grandparents who live on in memories: Gita, Joe, Renee and Sam. I love and cherish you all so very much.

I am also very grateful to all my friends and loved ones whom I think of as my 'extended family'. I can't name all of you, but here are a few special mentions. Itamar Shuval, Ore Goldgammer, Nadeem Noordin and Rikki Brest are among my oldest friends and have always believed in me since my earliest teenage years. My treasured 'sisters and brothers from other mothers', Catriona Boffard, Andrew Robinson and Dale Imerman. You all continue to play such important roles in my life for which I am so grateful. Kevin Croft and Ryan Sauer, my 'mastermind' partners, you have always been a rich source of ideas, inspiration and accountability. I also want to thank my travel companions with whom I've shared some special experiences all over the world, especially Howard Sackstein and Ran Neu-Ner. Lastly I must pay special thanks to my best friend and confidante, Angelique Daubermann, who has been so patient while I have often burnt the candle at both ends during the writing of this book. I'm a strong believer that we become most like the people we spend most of our time with, and I am honoured to be able to spend my time with all of you.

To my close team — Marc Wegkamp and Mishka Phillips — I want to say that your support and commitment to our shared vision has been a major factor in our recent success, and *will* be in our *future* success! You will always have my loyalty and support. Jossi Afargan, Ray Brown, Ryan Peimer and Daniel Peimer: you guys are unbelievably professional and reliable, and your support through the years has been unwavering despite almost every deadline being 'urgent' and everything always being needed 'yesterday'. Monty Nkosi: thank you for keeping my mind sharp and my body fit. Your focus and dedication always inspires me.

John Vlismas: I will always have time for you just as you have always had time for me. You have a remarkable way of seeing things differently from almost everyone else, and your willingness to add value to other people is inspiring.

Rina Broomberg: you have a calm conviction behind your beautiful smile, and have always been an open ear and firm supporter since we first met. Your vision and values rub off on everyone around you, and this shows in the amount of influence you naturally have with people.

Rabbi David Masinter: your passion for making a difference in the world brings out the best in people. This is evident in how many people support all the programmess you run that make such a difference in the lives of South Africans. You certainly know a thing or two about influence (and one day you will send me a quote on influence...)

Paul Malek and Vicus Cruywagen: since I was nine years old you two have been the leading lights of the magic scene in Johannesburg. I have learned so much from you and admire what you both continue to do for the art of magic in South Africa.

Gareth Cliff: through our interesting discussions both on and off air, raising funds together for charitable causes, and sharing a mutual friend or two, I have grown a deep respect for the efforts you make to influence the way forward in South Africa — from your pioneering business (ad)ventures, to your powerful campaigns to bring about change across the nation.

To my fellow conference speakers, trainers and entertainers: I am grateful to be able to call you my friends. I continue to learn so much from all of you both on and off the stage. Your motivation and professionalism keeps me energised and on my toes. I'm so proud to belong to a group of people who are changing people's lives globally, right from the bottom tip of Africa. There are too many of you to mention, but let me thank Justin Cohen, who has a great zest for life and for helping people to be the best versions of themselves; Shelley Walters, who has a heart of gold and equips so many people to present and share their own ideas so effectively; Cyrus Rogers, the man with the golden voice and a golden heart, who is always ready to help and support wherever he can; and Michael Jackson, who not only leads change in organisations but is positively changing the professional speaking circuit in South Africa.

Robert Cialdini, Daniel Kahneman, Dan Ariely, Stephen Dubner, Richard Wiseman, Derren Brown, Richard Osterlind, Banachek, Andy Nyman, Max Maven, Joshua Quinn, Colin McLeod, David Copperfield, Keith Barry, Pete Turner, John Maxwell and Malcolm Gladwell have all played a part, either directly or indirectly, in helping to shape my ideas as a mentalist.

To everyone who has ever featured me on their shows or in their newspapers, magazines and conversations — thank you! I wouldn't be able to reach hundreds of thousands of people annually without you helping to carrying my messages and my reputation to your audiences, friends and families. There is no point in becoming an expert in isolation. I am grateful to you for helping me to move forward through your circles of influence.

My clients, whether old or now, are all so very valuable to me. Without your support I would not be able to live my dream. If I try to remember as far back as I can, I cannot recall a single bad client. I know that this is something that not many people can say. For this, I am truly grateful.

Finally, I want to place on record my enormous thanks to Ian Rowland. Ian has contributed a great deal to the world of mentalism and cold reading, and I have learned a huge amount from his book as well as from our many phone calls and times spent together in London. Ian has helped me tremendously with this book, and I have benefited greatly from his expertise not only as a fellow mentalist but also as a highly talented (and fast!) writer. If you are interested in the themes in this book, I suggest you get in touch with Ian and study with him. It's money well spent. Also, if you're trying to write a book, and you need the help and expertise of a professional writer... Ian is *the* man!

About the author

Gilan Gork is an internationally acclaimed mentalist who regularly features on prime-time TV shows as well as in media interviews and press articles.

With more than eighteen year's professional experience, Gilan has been dubbed the Master of Influence.

Gilan's live mentalism shows look impressively psychic in nature! However, he never claims any supernatural powers — everything he does is achieved through a shrewd combination of psychology, sleight of mind and other skills he has spent a lifetime developing.

Gilan is in great demand as a corporate speaker and trainer. He shows businesspeople that being able to read and influence people is the key to success in leadership, sales, negotiation and other business contexts.

Made in the USA
Charleston, SC
06 July 2015